THE SIDEREAL MESSENGER

OF

GALILEO GALILEI

AND A PART OF THE PREFACE TO KEPLER'S DIOPTRICS

CONTAINING THE ORIGINAL ACCOUNT OF GALILEO'S
ASTRONOMICAL DISCOVERIES.

A Translation with Introduction and Notes

BY

EDWARD STAFFORD CARLOS, M.A.

HEAD MATHEMATICAL MASTER IN CHRIST'S HOSPITAL.

RIVINGTONS

WATERLOO PLACE, LONDON

Oxford and Cambridge

MDCCCLXXX

PREFATORY NOTE.

ABOUT five years ago I was engaged in preparing
a catalogue of the ancient books which belong to
Christ's Hospital.   One portion of these books
consisted of a collection of ancient mathematical
works presented at various times for the use of that
part of the school which is known as the Royal
Mathematical Foundation of King Charles II.
Amongst them were some well known by name to
every mathematical student, but which few have
ever seen.   Perhaps the most interesting of them
all was a little volume, printed in London in 1653,
containing Gassendi's *Explanation of the Ptolemaic
and Copernican Systems of Astronomy*, as well as
that of Tycho Brahe, Galileo's *Sidereus Nuncius*,
and Kepler's *Dioptrics*.   I found Galileo's account

of his astronomical discoveries so interesting, both in matter and in style, that I translated it as a recreation from school-work. I venture to think that others also will be interested in following Galileo through the apprehension of his famous discoveries, and in reading the language in which he announced them.

INTRODUCTION.

IN 1609, Galileo, then Professor of Mathematics at Padua, in the service of the Venetian Republic, heard from a correspondent at Paris of the invention of a telescope, and set to work to consider how such an instrument could be made. The result was his invention of the telescope known by his name, and identical in principle with the modern operaglass. In a maritime and warlike State, the advantages to be expected from such an invention were immediately recognised, and Galileo was rewarded with a confirmation of his Professorship for life, and a handsome stipend, in recognition of his invention and construction of the first telescope seen at Venice. In his pamphlet, *The Sidereal Messenger,* here translated, Galileo relates how he came to learn the value of the telescope for astronomical research; and how his observations were rewarded by numerous discoveries in rapid succession, and at length by that of Jupiter's satellites. Galileo at once saw the value of this discovery as bearing upon the establishment of the Copernican system of astronomy, which had met with slight acceptance, and indeed as yet had hardly any recommendation except that of greater simplicity. Kepler had just published at Prague his work on the planet Mars (*Commentaria de motibus Stellæ Martis*), on which he had been engaged apparently for eight years; there he heard of Galileo's discoveries, and at length was invited by Galileo himself, through a common friend, Giuliano de' Medici, ambassador of the Grand-Duke of Tuscany, Cosmo de' Medici II., to the Emperor Rudolph II., to correspond with Galileo on the subject of these discoveries. The Emperor also requested his opinion, and Kepler accordingly examined Galileo's *Sidereal Messenger* in a pamphlet, entitled *A Discussion with the Sidereal Messenger* (Florence, 1610).

In this *Discussion* Kepler gives reasons for accepting Galileo's observations—although he was not able to verify them from want of a telescope—and entirely supports Galileo's views and conclusions, adducing his own previous speculations, or pointing out, as in the case of Galileo's idea of earth-light on the moon, the previous conception of

the same explanation of the phenomenon. He
rejects, however, Galileo's explanation of the copper
colour of the moon in eclipses. Kepler ends by
expressing unbounded enthusiasm at the discovery
of Jupiter's satellites, and the argument it furnishes
in support of the Copernican theory.

Soon after, in 1611, Kepler published another
pamphlet, his *Narrative*, giving an account of actual
observations made in verification of Galileo's discoveries by himself and several friends, whose
names he gives, with a telescope made by Galileo,
and belonging to Ernest, Elector and Archbishop
of Cologne. Kepler and his friends saw the lunar
mountains and three of the satellites of Jupiter, but
failed to make out any signs of the ring of Saturn
corresponding to the imperfect description of
Galileo.

Kepler had previously published a treatise on
Optics (Frankfort, 1604). He now extended it to
the consideration of the theory of the telescope, and
explained the principle of Galileo's telescope; he
also showed another combination of lenses which
would produce a similar effect. This was the principle of the common astronomical telescope, often
called, from this circumstance, Kepler's telescope,
though he did not construct it. The account of

Galileo's later astronomical discoveries of Saturn's
ring and the phases of Venus is taken from the
preface of this work.—(Kepler's *Dioptrics;* Augsburg, 1611.)

In 1612 Galileo published a series of observations
of solar spots, and in 1618 some observations of
three comets.   There exist also long series of
minute observations of Jupiter and his satellites,
continued to November 1619.—(Galileo's *Works;*
Florence, 1845.)

Further astronomical researches may have been
hindered by failing sight.   One more astronomical
discovery, however, that of the moon's librations,
was made as late as 1637, and the announcement
of it is dated "dalla mia carcere di Arcetri."
Galileo died January 8, 1642.

The following editions have been used for the
translation :—
    Galileo's *Works.*
        1. Florence, 1718.
        2. Padua, 1744.
        3. Florence, 1842-56.
    Sidereus Nuncius.
        1. Venice, 1610.
        2. London, 1653.

Kepler's *Works,* ed. C. Frisch. Frankfurt a. M., 1858-71.

Prodromus dissertationum mathematicarum continens Mysterium Cosmographicum de admirabili proportione orbium cœlestium. Tübingen, 1596.

Astronomia nova αἰτιολογητός (Commentaria de motibus stellæ Martis). [Prague,] 1609.

THE

SIDEREAL MESSENGER

OF

GALILEO GALILEI

THE
SIDEREAL MESSENGER

*UNFOLDING GREAT AND MARVELLOUS SIGHTS,
AND PROPOSING THEM TO THE ATTENTION OF EVERY ONE,
BUT ESPECIALLY PHILOSOPHERS AND ASTRONOMERS,*

BEING SUCH AS HAVE BEEN OBSERVED BY

GALILEO GALILEI

A GENTLEMAN OF FLORENCE,
PROFESSOR OF MATHEMATICS IN THE UNIVERSITY OF PADUA,

WITH THE AID OF A

TELESCOPE

lately invented by him,

*Respecting the Moon's Surface, an innumerable number of Fixed Stars,
the Milky Way, and Nebulous Stars, but especially respecting
Four Planets which revolve round the Planet Jupiter at
different distances and in different periodic times, with
amazing velocity, and which, after remaining
unknown to every one up to this day, the
Author recently discovered, and
determined to name the*

MEDICEAN STARS.

VENICE 1610.

COSMO DE' MEDICI, THE SECOND,

FOURTH GRAND-DUKE OF TUSCANY.

THERE is certainly something very noble and large-minded in the intention of those who have endeavoured to protect from envy the noble achievements of distinguished men, and to rescue their names, worthy of immortality, from oblivion and decay. This desire has given us the lineaments of famous men, sculptured in marble, or fashioned in bronze, as a memorial of them to future ages ; to the same feeling we owe the erection of statues, both ordinary and equestrian; hence, as the poet[1] says, has originated expenditure, mounting to the stars, upon columns and pyramids; with this desire, lastly, cities have been built, and distinguished by the names of those men, whom the gratitude of posterity thought worthy of being handed down to all ages.   For the state of the human mind is such, that

---

[1] Propertius, iii. 2. 17–22.

A

unless it be continually stirred by the counterparts[1] of matters, obtruding themselves upon it from without, all recollection of the matters easily passes away from it.

But others, having regard for more stable and more lasting monuments, secured the eternity of the fame of great men by placing it under the protection, not of marble or bronze, but of the Muses' guardianship and the imperishable monuments of literature. But why do I mention these things, as if human wit, content with these regions, did not dare to advance further; whereas, since she well understood that all human monuments do perish at last by violence, by weather, or by age, she took a wider view, and invented more imperishable signs, over which destroying Time and envious Age could claim no rights; so, betaking herself to the sky, she inscribed on the well-known orbs of the brightest stars—those everlasting orbs—the names of those who, for eminent and god-like deeds, were accounted worthy to enjoy an eternity in company with the stars. Wherefore the fame of Jupiter, Mars, Mercury, Hercules, and the rest of the heroes by whose names the stars are called, will not fade

---

[1] Compare Lucretius iv. 881 :
　　　 Dico animo nostro primum simulacra meandi
　　　 Accidere, atque animum pulsare.

until the extinction of the splendour of the constellations themselves.

But this invention of human shrewdness, so particularly noble and admirable, has gone out of date ages ago, inasmuch as primeval heroes are in possession of those bright abodes, and keep them by a sort of right; into whose company the affection of Augustus in vain attempted to introduce Julius Cæsar; for when he wished that the name of the Julian constellation should be given to a star, which appeared in his time, one of those which the Greeks and the Latins alike name, from their hair-like tails, comets, it vanished in a short time and mocked his too eager hope. But we are able to read the heavens for your highness, most Serene Prince, far more truly and more happily, for scarcely have the immortal graces of your mind begun to shine on earth, when bright stars present themselves in the heavens, like tongues to tell and celebrate your most surpassing virtues to all time. Behold therefore, four stars reserved for your famous name, and those not belonging to the common and less conspicuous multitude of fixed stars, but in the bright ranks of the planets—four stars which, moving differently from each other, round the planet Jupiter, the most glorious of all the planets, as if they were his own children,

accomplish the courses of their orbits with marvellous
velocity, while all the while with one accord they
complete all together mighty revolutions every ten
years round the centre of the universe, that is, round
the SUN.

But the Maker of the Stars himself seemed to direct
me by clear reasons to assign these new planets to the
famous name of your highness in preference to all
others. For just as these stars, like children worthy
of their sire, never leave the side of Jupiter by any
appreciable distance, so who does not know that
clemency, kindness of heart, gentleness of manners,
splendour of royal blood, nobleness in public functions,
wide extent of influence and power over others, all
of which have fixed their common abode and seat in
your highness,—who, I say, does not know that all
these qualities, according to the providence of God,
from whom all good things do come, emanate from
the benign star of Jupiter? Jupiter, Jupiter, I
maintain, at the instant of the birth of your highness
having at length emerged from the turbid mists of
the horizon, and being in possession of the middle
quarter of the heavens, and illuminating the eastern
angle, from his own royal house, from that exalted
throne, looked out upon your most happy birth, and
poured forth into a most pure atmosphere all the

brightness of his majesty, in order that your tender body and your mind—though that was already adorned by God with still more splendid graces—might imbibe with your first breath the whole of that influence and power. But why should I use only plausible arguments when I can almost absolutely demonstrate my conclusion? It was the will of Almighty God that I should be judged by your most serene parents not unworthy to be employed in teaching your highness mathematics, which duty I discharged, during the four years just passed, at that time of the year when it is customary to take a relaxation from severer studies. Wherefore, since it evidently fell to my lot by God's will, to serve your highness, and so to receive the rays of your surpassing clemency and beneficence in a position near your person, what wonder is it if you have so warmed my heart that it thinks about scarcely anything else day and night, but how I, who am indeed your subject not only by inclination, but also by my very birth and lineage, may be known to be most anxious for your glory, and most grateful to you? And so, inasmuch as under your patronage, most serene Cosmo, I have discovered these stars, which were unknown to all astronomers before me, I have, with very good right, determined to designate them with the most august name of your family. And as

I was the first to investigate them, who can rightly blame me if I give them a name, and call them *the Medicean Stars*, hoping that as much consideration may accrue to these stars from this title, as other stars have brought to other heroes? For not to speak of your most serene ancestors, to whose everlasting glory the monuments of all history bear witness, your virtue alone, most mighty sire, can confer on those stars an immortal name ; for who can doubt that you will not only maintain and preserve the expectations, high though they be, about yourself, which you have aroused by the very happy beginning of your government, but that you will also far surpass them, so that when you have conquered others like yourself, you may still vie with yourself, and become day by day greater than yourself and your greatness ?

Accept, then, most clement Prince, this addition to the glory of your family, reserved by the stars for you ; and may you enjoy for many years those good blessings, which are sent to you not so much from the stars as from God, the Maker and Governor of the stars.

Your Highness's most devoted servant,

GALILEO GALILEI.

PADUA, *March* 12, 1610.

THE ASTRONOMICAL MESSENGER

*Containing and setting forth Observations lately made with the
aid of a newly invented* TELESCOPE *respecting the Moon's
Surface, the Milky Way, Nebulous Stars, an
innumerable multitude of Fixed Stars, and
also respecting Four Planets never before
seen, which have been named*

THE COSMIAN STARS.[1]

IN the present small treatise I set forth some matters
of great interest for all observers of natural phenomena to look at and consider. They are of great
interest, I think, first, from their intrinsic excellence ;
secondly, from their absolute novelty ; and lastly, also
on account of the instrument by the aid of which
they have been presented to my apprehension.

The number of the Fixed Stars which observers
have been able to see without artificial powers of
sight up to this day can be counted. It is therefore

---

[1] The satellites of Jupiter are here called " *the Cosmian Stars* " in honour
of Cosmo de' Medici, but elsewhere Galileo calls them " *the Medicean
Stars.*" Kepler sometimes calls them " *the Medicean Stars,*" but more
often " *satellites.*"

decidedly a great feat to add to their number, and to set distinctly before the eyes other stars in myriads, which have never been seen before, and which surpass the old, previously known, stars in number more than ten times.

Again, it is a most beautiful and delightful sight to behold the body of the Moon, which is distant from us nearly sixty *semi*-diameters[1] of the Earth, as near as if it was at a distance of only two of the same measures; so that the diameter of this same Moon appears about thirty times larger, its surface about nine hundred times, and its solid mass nearly 27,000 times larger than when it is viewed only with the naked eye; and consequently any one may know with the certainty that is due to the use of our senses, that the Moon certainly does not possess a smooth and polished surface, but one rough and uneven, and, just like the face of the Earth itself, is everywhere full of vast protuberances, deep chasms, and sinuosities.

Then to have got rid of disputes about the Galaxy or Milky Way, and to have made its nature clear to the very senses, not to say to the understanding,

---

[1] Galileo says, " per sex denas fere terrestres *diametros* a nobis remotum" by mistake for *semi-diametros*, and the same mistake occurs in p. 11.

seems by no means a matter which ought to be considered of slight importance. In addition to this, to point out, as with one's finger, the nature of those stars which every one of the astronomers up to this time has called *nebulous*, and to demonstrate that it is very different from what has hitherto been believed, will be pleasant, and very fine. But that which will excite the greatest astonishment by far, and which indeed especially moved me to call the attention of all astronomers and philosophers, is this, namely, that I have discovered four planets, neither known nor observed by any one of the astronomers before my time, which have their orbits round a certain bright star, one of those previously known, like Venus and Mercury round the Sun, and are sometimes in front of it, sometimes behind it, though they never depart from it beyond certain limits. All which facts were discovered and observed a few days ago by the help of a telescope [1] devised by me, through God's grace first enlightening my mind.

Perchance other discoveries still more excellent will be made from time to time by me or by other

---

[1] The words used by Galileo for "telescope" are *perspicillum, specillum instrumentum, organum,* and *occhiale* (Ital.). Kepler uses also *oculare tubus, arundo dioptrica.* The word "*telescopium*" is used by Gassendi, 1647.

observers, with the assistance of a similar instrument, so I will first briefly record its shape and preparation, as well as the occasion of its being devised, and then I will give an account of the observations made by me.

Galileo's account of the invention of his telescope.

About ten months ago a report reached my ears that a Dutchman had constructed a telescope, by the aid of which visible objects, although at a great distance from the eye of the observer, were seen distinctly as if near; and some proofs of its most wonderful performances were reported, which some gave credence to, but others contradicted. A few days after, I received confirmation of the report in a letter written from Paris by a noble Frenchman, Jaques Badovere, which finally determined me to give myself up first to inquire into the principle of the telescope, and then to consider the means by which I might compass the invention of a similar instrument, which a little while after I succeeded in doing, through deep study of the theory of Refraction; and I prepared a tube, at first of lead, in the ends of which I fitted two glass lenses, both plane on one side, but on the other side one spherically convex, and the other concave. Then bringing my eye to the concave lens I saw objects satisfactorily large and near, for they appeared one-third of the distance off and nine times larger than when they are seen with the natural eye alone. I shortly afterwards constructed another telescope with more nicety, which magnified objects more than sixty times. At length, by sparing neither labour nor expense, I succeeded in constructing for myself an instrument so superior that objects seen through it appear magnified nearly a thousand times, and more than thirty times nearer than if viewed by the natural powers of sight alone.

It would be altogether a waste of time to enumerate the number and importance of the benefits which this instrument may be expected to confer, when used by land or sea. But without paying attention to its use for terrestrial objects, I betook myself to observations of the heavenly bodies; and first of all, I viewed the Moon as near as if it was scarcely two *semi*-diameters[1] of the Earth distant. After the Moon, I frequently observed other heavenly bodies, both fixed stars and planets, with incredible delight; and, when I saw their very great number, I began to consider about a method by which I might be able to measure their distances apart, and at length I found one. And here it is fitting that all who intend to

Galileo's first observations with his telescope.

---

[1] " Vix per duas Telluris *diametros*," by mistake for " semi-diametros."

turn their attention to observations of this kind should receive certain cautions.   For, in the first place, it is absolutely necessary for them to prepare a most perfect telescope, one which will show very bright objects distinct and free from any mistiness, and will magnify them at least 400 times, for then it will show them as if only one-twentieth of their distance off.   For unless the instrument be of such power, it will be in vain to attempt to view all the things which have been seen by me in the heavens, or which will be enumerated hereafter.

Method of determining the magnifying power of the telescope.

But in order that any one may be a little more certain about the magnifying power of his instrument, he shall fashion two circles, or two square pieces of paper, one of which is 400 times greater than the other, but that will be when the diameter of the greater is twenty times the length of the diameter of the other.   Then he shall view from a distance simultaneously both surfaces, fixed on the same wall, the smaller with one eye applied to the telescope, and the larger with the other eye unassisted; for that may be done without inconvenience at one and the same instant with both eyes open.   Then both figures will appear of the same size, if the instrument magnifies objects in the desired proportion.

After such an instrument has been prepared, the

method of measuring distances remains for inquiry, and this we shall accomplish by the following contrivance :—

For the sake of being more easily understood, I will suppose a tube A B C D.[1]   Let E be the eye of the observer ; then, when there are no lenses in the tube rays from the eye to the object F G would be drawn in the straight lines E C F, E D G, but when the lenses have been inserted, let the rays go in the bent lines E C H, E D I,—for they are contracted, and those which originally, when unaffected by the lenses, were directed to the object F G, will

---

1

The line C H in Galileo's figure represents the small pencil of rays from H which, after refraction through the telescope, reach the eye E. The enlarged figure shows that if O P be the radius of the aperture employed, the point H of the object would be just outside the field of view.   The method, however, is at best only a very rough one, as the boundary of the field of view in this telescope is unavoidably indistinct.

include only the part H I. Hence the ratio of the distance E H to the line H I being known, we shall be able to find, by means of a table of sines, the magnitude of the angle subtended at the eye by the object H I, which we shall find to contain only some minutes. But if we fit on the lens C D thin plates of metal, pierced, some with larger, others with smaller apertures, by putting on over the lens sometimes one plate, sometimes another, as may be necessary, we shall construct at our pleasure different subtending angles of more or fewer minutes, by the help of which we shall be able to measure conveniently the intervals between stars separated ·by an angular distance of some minutes, within an error of one or two minutes. But let it suffice for the present to have thus slightly touched, and as it were just put our lips to these matters, for on some other opportunity I will publish the theory of this instrument in completeness.

Now let me review the observations made by me during the two months just past, again inviting the attention of all who are eager for true philosophy to the beginnings which led to the sight of most important phenomena.

The Moon. Ruggedness of its surface. Let me speak first of the surface of the Moon, which is turned towards us. For the sake of being understood more easily, I distinguish two parts in it, which I call respectively the brighter and the darker. The brighter part seems to surround and pervade the whole hemisphere ; but the darker part, like a sort of cloud, discolours the Moon's surface and makes it appear covered with spots. Now these spots, as they are somewhat dark and of considerable size, are plain to every one, and every age has seen them, wherefore I shall call them *great* or *ancient* spots, to distinguish them from other spots, smaller in size, but so thickly scattered that they sprinkle the whole surface of the Moon, but especially the brighter portion of it. These spots have never been observed by any one before me ; and from my observations of them, often repeated, I have been led to that opinion which I have expressed, namely, that I feel sure that the surface of the Moon is not perfectly smooth, free from in-equalities and exactly spherical, as a large school of philosophers considers with regard to the Moon and the other heavenly bodies, but that, on the contrary, it is full of inequalities, uneven, full of hollows and protuberances, just like the surface of the Earth itself, which is varied everywhere by lofty mountains and deep valleys.

The appearances from which we may gather these conclusions are of the following nature :—On the fourth or fifth day after new-moon, when the Moon presents itself to us with bright horns, the boundary which divides the part in shadow from the enlightened part does not extend continuously in an ellipse, as would happen in the case of a perfectly spherical body, but it is marked out by an irregular, uneven, and very wavy line, as represented in the figure given, for several bright excrescences, as they may be called, extend beyond the boundary of light and shadow into the dark part, and on the other hand pieces of shadow encroach upon the light :—nay, even a great quantity of small blackish spots, altogether separated from the dark part, sprinkle everywhere almost the whole space which is at the time flooded with the Sun's light, with the exception of that part alone which is occupied by the great and ancient spots. I have noticed that the small spots just mentioned have this common characteristic always and in every case, that they have the dark part towards the Sun's position, and on the side away from the Sun they have brighter boundaries, as if they were crowned with shining summits. Now we have an appearance quite similar on the Earth about sunrise, when we behold the valleys, not yet flooded with light, but the mountains surrounding them on the side opposite to the Sun already ablaze with the splendour of his

Sketches by Galileo to show

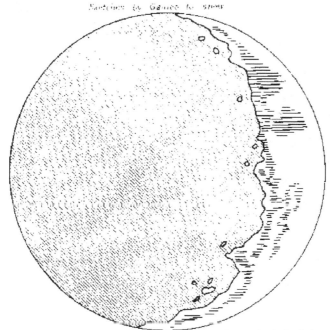

the indentation of the terminator and illuminated summits of mountains in the dark part of the moon.

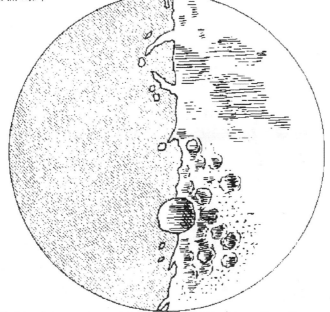

the shape of a lunar mountain and of a walled plain   Galileo Sidereus Nuncius, Venice 1610.

beams; and just as the shadows in the hollows of the Earth diminish in size as the Sun rises higher, so also these spots on the Moon lose their blackness as the illuminated part grows larger and larger. Again, not only are the boundaries of light and shadow in the Moon seen to be uneven and sinuous, but—and this produces still greater astonishment—there appear very many bright points within the darkened portion of the Moon, altogether divided and broken off from the illuminated tract, and separated from it by no inconsiderable interval, which, after a little while, gradually increase in size and brightness, and after an hour or two become joined on to the rest of the bright portion, now become somewhat larger; but in the meantime others, one here and another there, shooting up as if growing, are lighted up within the shaded portion, increase in size, and at last are linked on to the same luminous surface, now still more extended. An example of this is given in the same figure. Now, is it not the case on the Earth before sunrise, that while the level plain is still in shadow, the peaks of the most lofty mountains are illuminated by the Sun's rays? After a little while does not the light spread further, while the middle and larger parts of those mountains are becoming illuminated; and at length, when the Sun has risen, do not the illuminated parts

B

of the plains and hills join together ?   The grandeur,
however, of such prominences and depressions in the
Moon seems to surpass both in magnitude and extent
the ruggedness of the Earth's surface, as I shall hereafter show.   And here I cannot refrain from mention-
ing what a remarkable spectacle I observed while the
Moon was rapidly approaching her first quarter, a
representation of which is given in the same illustration, placed opposite page 16.   A protuberance of the
shadow, of great size, indented the illuminated part in
the neighbourhood of the lower cusp ; and when I had
observed this indentation longer, and had seen that it
was dark throughout, at length, after about two hours,
a bright peak began to arise a little below the middle
of the depression ; this by degrees increased, and
presented a triangular shape, but was as yet quite
detached and separated from the illuminated surface.
Soon around it three other small points began to
shine, until, when the Moon was just about to set,
that triangular figure, having now extended and
widened, began to be connected with the rest of the
illuminated part, and, still girt with the three bright
peaks already mentioned, suddenly burst into the
indentation of shadow like a vast promontory of
light.

At the ends of the upper and lower cusps also

certain bright points, quite away from the rest of the bright part, began to rise out of the shadow, as is seen depicted in the same illustration.

In both horns also, but especially in the lower one, there was a great quantity of dark spots, of which those which are nearer the boundary of light and shadow appear larger and darker, but those which are more remote less dark and more indistinct. In all cases, however, just as I have mentioned before, the dark portion of the spot faces the position of the Sun's illumination, and a brighter edge surrounds the darkened spot on the side away from the Sun, and towards the region of the Moon in shadow. This part of the surface of the Moon, where it is marked with spots like a peacock's tail with its azure eyes, is rendered like those glass vases which, through being plunged while still hot from the kiln into cold water, acquire a crackled and wavy surface, from which circumstance they are commonly called *frosted glasses.*[1]

Now the great spots of the Moon observed at the same time are not seen to be at all similarly broken, or full of depressions and prominences, but rather to be even and uniform; for only here and there some spaces, rather brighter than the rest, crop up; so that if any

The lunar spots are suggested to be possibly seas bordered by ranges of mountains.

[1] Specimens of *frosted or crackled Venetian glass* are to be seen in the Slade Collection, British Museum, and fully justify Galileo's comparison.

one wishes to revive the old opinion of the Pytha-
goreans, that the Moon is another Earth, so to say,
the brighter portion may very fitly represent the
surface of the land, and the darker the expanse of
water.   Indeed, I have never doubted that if the
sphere of the Earth were seen from a distance, when
flooded with the Sun's rays, that part of the surface
which is land would present itself to view as brighter,
and that which is water as darker in comparison.
Moreover, the great spots in the Moon are seen to be
more depressed than the brighter tracts ; for in the
Moon, both when crescent and when waning, on the
boundary between the light and shadow, which pro-
jects in some places round the great spots, the adjacent
regions are always brighter, as I have noticed in
drawing my illustrations, and the edges of the spots
referred to are not only more depressed than the
brighter parts, but are more even, and are not broken
by ridges or ruggednesses.   But the brighter part
stands out most near the spots, so that both before
the first quarter and about the third quarter also,
around a certain spot in the upper part of the figure,
that is, occupying the northern region of the Moon,
some vast prominences on the upper and lower sides
of it rise to an enormous elevation, as the illustrations
show.   This same spot before the third quarter is seen

to be walled round with boundaries of a deeper shade, which just like very lofty mountain summits appear darker on the side away from the Sun, and brighter on the side where they face the Sun ; but in the case of the cavities the opposite happens, for the part of them away from the Sun appears brilliant, and that part which lies nearer to the Sun dark and in shadow. After a time, when the enlightened portion of the Moon's surface has diminished in size, as soon as the whole or nearly so of the spot already mentioned is covered with shadow, the brighter ridges of the mountains mount high above the shade. These two appearances are shown in the illustrations which are given.

There is one other point which I must on no account forget, which I have noticed and rather wondered at. It is this :—The middle of the Moon, as it seems, is occupied by a certain cavity larger than all the rest, and in shape perfectly round. I have looked at this depression near both the first and third quarters, and I have represented it as well as I can in the second illustration already given. It produces the same appearance as to effects of light and shade as a tract like Bohemia would produce on the Earth,

Description of a lunar crater, perhaps Tycho.[1]

---

[1] Webb, *Celestial Objects for Common Telescopes*, p. 104, suggests this identification.

if it were shut in on all sides by very lofty mountains arranged on the circumference of a perfect
circle; for the tract in the Moon is walled in with
peaks of such enormous height that the furthest side
adjacent to the dark portion of the Moon is seen
bathed in sunlight before the boundary between
light and shade reaches half-way across the circular
space. But according to the characteristic property
of the rest of the spots, the shaded portion of this too
faces the Sun, and the bright part is towards the dark
side of the Moon, which for the third time I advise to
be carefully noticed as a most solid proof of the
ruggednesses and unevennesses spread over the whole
of the bright region of the Moon. Of these spots,
moreover, the darkest are always those which are
near to the boundary-line between the light and the
shadow, but those further off appear both smaller in
size and less decidedly dark; so that at length, when
the Moon at opposition becomes full, the darkness of
the cavities differs from the brightness of the prominences with a subdued and very slight difference.

Reasons for
believing
that there is a
difference of
constitution
in various
parts of the
Moon's sur-
face.

These phenomena which we have reviewed are
observed in the bright tracts of the Moon. In the
great spots we do not see such differences of depressions and prominences as we are compelled to recognise in the brighter parts, owing to the change of their

shapes under different degrees of illumination by the
Sun's rays according to the manifold variety of the
Sun's position with regard to the Moon.   Still, in the
great spots there do exist some spaces rather less
dark than the rest, as I have noted in the illustrations,
but these spaces always have the same appearance,
and the depth of their shadow is neither intensified
nor diminished ; they do appear indeed sometimes a
little more shaded, sometimes a little less, but the
change of colour is very slight, according as the Sun's
rays fall upon them more or less obliquely ; and
besides, they are joined to the adjacent parts of the
spots with a very gradual connection, so that their
boundaries mingle and melt into the surrounding
region.   But it is quite different with the spots which
occupy the brighter parts of the Moon's surface, for,
just as if they were precipitous crags with numerous
rugged and jagged peaks, they have well-defined
boundaries through the sharp contrast of light and
shade.   Moreover, inside those great spots certain
other tracts are seen brighter than the surrounding
region, and some of them very bright indeed, but
the appearance of these, as well as of the darker parts,
is always the same ; there is no change of shape or
brightness or depth of shadow, so that it becomes a
matter of certainty and beyond doubt that their

appearance is owing to real dissimilarity of parts, and
not to unevennesses only in their configuration, changing in different ways the shadows of the same parts
according to the variations of their illumination by the
Sun, which really happens in the case of the other
smaller spots occupying the brighter portion of the
Moon, for day by day they change, increase, decrease,
or disappear, inasmuch as they derive their origin
only from the shadows of prominences.

Explanation of the even-ness of the illuminated part of the circumfer-ence of the Moon's orb by the ana-logy of terres-trial pheno-mena, or by a possible lunar atmo-sphere.

But here I feel that some people may be troubled
with grave doubt, and perhaps seized with a difficulty
so serious as to compel them to feel uncertain about
the conclusion just explained and supported by so
many phenomena. For if that part of the Moon's
surface which reflects the Sun's rays most brightly is
full of sinuosities, protuberances, and cavities innumerable, why, when the Moon is increasing, does the outer
edge which looks toward the west, when the Moon is
waning, the other half-circumference towards the east,
and at full-moon the whole circle, appear not uneven,
rugged, and irregular, but perfectly round and circular,
as sharply defined as if marked out with a pair of
compasses, and without the indentations of any protuberances or cavities? And most remarkably so,
because the whole unbroken edge belongs to that part
of the Moon's surface which possesses the property of

appearing brighter than the rest, which I have said to be throughout full of protuberances and cavities. For not one of the Great Spots extends quite to the circumference, but all of them are seen to be together away from the edge. Of this phenomenon, which affords a handle for such serious doubt, I produce two causes, and so two solutions of the difficulty.

The first solution which I offer is this :—If the protuberances and cavities in the body of the Moon existed only on the edge of the circle that bounds the hemisphere which we see, then the Moon might, or rather must, show itself to us with the appearance of a toothed wheel, being bounded with an irregular and uneven circumference ; but if, instead of a single set of prominences arranged along the actual circumference only, very many ranges of mountains with their cavities and ruggednesses are set one behind the other along the extreme edge of the Moon, and that too not only in the hemisphere which we see, but also in that which is turned away from us, but still near the boundary of the hemisphere, then the eye, viewing them afar off, will not at all be able to detect the differences of prominences and cavities, for the intervals between the mountains situated in the same circle, or in the same chain, are hidden by the jutting forward of other prominences situated in other ranges,

and especially if the eye of the observer is placed in
the same line with the tops of the prominences mentioned.   So on the Earth, the summits of a number of
mountains close together appear situated in one plane,
if the spectator is a long way off and standing at the
same elevation.   So when the sea is rough, the tops of
the waves seem to form one plane, although between
the billows there is many a gulf and chasm, so deep
that not only the hulls, but even the bulwarks, masts,
and sails of stately ships are hidden amongst them.
Therefore, as within the Moon, as well as round her
circumference, there is a manifold arrangement of
prominences and cavities, and the eye, regarding them
from a great distance, is placed in nearly the same
plane with their summits, no one need think it strange
that they present themselves to the visual ray which
just grazes them as an unbroken line quite free from
unevennesses.   To this explanation may be added
another, namely, that there is round the body of the
Moon, just as round the Earth, an envelope of some
substance denser than the rest of the ether, which is
sufficient to receive and reflect the Sun's rays, although
it does not possess so much opaqueness as to be able
to prevent our seeing through it—especially when it
is not illuminated.   That envelope, when illuminated
by the Sun's rays, renders the body of the Moon

apparently larger than it really is, and would be able
to stop our sight from penetrating to the solid body
of the Moon, if its thickness were greater; now, it is
of greater thickness about the circumference of the
Moon, greater, I mean, not in actual thickness, but
with reference to our sight-rays, which cut it obliquely;
and so it may stop our vision, especially when it is
in a state of brightness, and may conceal the true
circumference of the Moon on the side towards the
Sun.

This may be understood more clearly from the
adjoining figure, in which the body of the Moon, A B C,

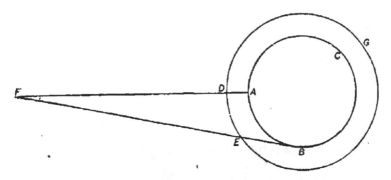

is surrounded by an enveloping atmosphere, D E G.
An eye at F penetrates to the middle parts of the
Moon, as at A, through a thickness, D A, of the atmosphere; but towards the extreme parts a mass of
atmosphere of greater depth, E B, shuts out its boundary from our sight. An argument in favour of this

is, that the illuminated portion of the Moon appears of larger circumference than the rest of the orb which is in shadow.

Perhaps also some will think that this same cause affords a very reasonable explanation why the greater spots on the Moon are not seen to reach to the edge of the circumference on any side, although it might be expected that some would be found about the edge as well as elsewhere; and it seems credible that there are spots there, but that they cannot be seen because they are hidden by a mass of atmosphere too thick and too bright for the sight to penetrate.

Calculation to show that the height of some lunar mountains exceeds four Italian miles* (22,000 British feet).

I think that it has been sufficiently made clear, from the explanation of phenomena which have been given, that the brighter part of the Moon's surface is dotted everywhere with protuberances and cavities; it only remains for me to speak about their size, and to show that the ruggednesses of the Earth's surface are far smaller than those of the Moon's; smaller, I mean, absolutely, so to say, and not only smaller in proportion to the size of the orbs on which they are. And this is plainly shown thus :—As I often observed in various positions of the Moon with reference to the

---

* In the list of the heights of lunar mountains determined by Beer and Maedler, given in their work *Der Mond* (Berlin, 1837), there are six which exceed 3000 toises, or 19,000 British feet.

Sun, that some summits within the portion of the
Moon in shadow appeared illumined, although at
some distance from the boundary of the light (the
terminator), by comparing their distance with the
complete diameter of the Moon, I learnt that it sometimes exceeded the one-twentieth $(\frac{1}{20}$th) part of the
diameter. Suppose the dis-
tance to be exactly $\frac{1}{20}$th
part of the diameter, and let
the diagram represent the
Moon's orb, of which C A F is
a great circle, ɪɪ its centre,
and C F a diameter, which
consequently bears to the
diameter of the Earth the

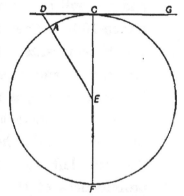

ratio 2 : 7; and since the diameter of the Earth, according to the most exact observations, contains 7000
Italian miles, C F will be 2000, and C E 1000, and the
$\frac{1}{20}$th part of the whole, C F, 100 miles. Also let C F
be a diameter of the great circle which divides the
bright part of the Moon from the dark part (for,
owing to the very great distance of the Sun from the
Moon this circle does not differ sensibly from a great
one), and let the distance of A from the point C be
$\frac{1}{20}$th part of that diameter; let the radius E A be
drawn, and let it be produced to cut the tangent line

G C D, which represents the ray that illumines the summit, in the point D. Then the arc C A or the straight line C D will be 100 of such units, as C E contains 1000. The sum of the squares of D C, C E is therefore 1,010,000, and the square of D E is equal to this; therefore the whole E D will be more than 1004; and A D will be more than 4 of such units, as C E contained 1000. Therefore the height of A D in the Moon, which represents a summit reaching up to the Sun's ray, G C D, and separated from the extremity C by the distance C D, is more than 4 Italian miles; but in the Earth there are no mountains which reach to the perpendicular height even of one mile. We are therefore left to conclude that it is clear that the prominences of the Moon are loftier than those of the Earth.

The faint illumination of the Moon's disc about new-moon explained to be due to earth-light.

I wish in this place to assign the cause of another lunar phenomenon well worthy of notice, and although this phenomenon was observed by me not lately, but many years ago, and has been pointed out to some of my intimate friends and pupils, explained, and assigned to its true cause, yet as the observation of it is rendered easier and more vivid by the help of a telescope, I have considered that it would not be unsuitably introduced in this place, but I wish to introduce it chiefly in order that the connection and resemblance between the Moon and the Earth may appear more plainly.

When the Moon, both before and after conjunction, is found not far from the Sun, not only does its orb show itself to our sight on the side where it is furnished with shining horns, but a slight and faint circumference is also seen to mark out the circle of the dark part, that part, namely, which is turned away from the Sun, and to separate it from the darker background of the sky.   But if we examine the matter more closely, we shall see that not only is the extreme edge of the part in shadow shining with a faint brightness, but that the entire face of the Moon, that side, that is, which does not feel the Sun's glare, is illuminated with a pale light of considerable brightness.   At the first glance only a fine circumference appears shining, on account of the darker part of the sky adjacent to it; whereas, on the contrary, the rest of the surface appears dark, on account of the contiguity of the shining horns, which destroys the clearness of our sight.   But if any one chooses such a position for himself, that by the interposition of a roof, or a chimney, or some other object between his sight and the Moon, but at a considerable distance from his eye, the shining horns are hidden, and the rest of the Moon's orb is left exposed to his view,

then he will find that this tract of the Moon also,
although deprived of sunlight, gleams with considerable light, and particularly so if the gloom of the
night has already deepened through the absence of
the Sun; for with a darker background the same
light appears brighter.   Moreover, it is found that
this secondary brightness of the Moon, as I may call
it, is greater in proportion as the Moon is less distant
from the Sun; for it abates more and more in proportion to the Moon's distance from that body, so
much so that after the first quarter, and before the .
end of the second, it is found to be weak and very
faint, although it be observed in a darker sky;
whereas, at an angular distance of 60° or less, even
during twilight, it is wonderfully bright, so bright
indeed that, with the help of a good telescope, the
great spots may be distinguished in it.

   This strange brightness has afforded no small per-
plexity to philosophical minds; and some have
published one thing, some another, as the cause to
be alleged for it.   Some have said that it is the
inherent and natural brightness of the Moon; some
that it is imparted to that body by the planet Venus;
or, as others maintain, by all the stars; while some
have said that it comes from the Sun, whose rays,
they say, find a way through the solid mass of the

Moon. But statements of this kind are disproved without much difficulty, and convincingly . demonstrated to be false. For if this kind of light were the Moon's own, or were contributed by the stars, the Moon would retain it, particularly in eclipses, and would show it then, when left in an unusually dark sky, but this is contrary to experience. For the brightness which is seen on the Moon in eclipses is far less intense, being somewhat reddish, and almost copper-coloured, whereas this is brighter and whiter; besides, the brightness seen during an eclipse is changeable and shifting, for it wanders over the face of the Moon, so that that part which is near the circumference of the circle of shadow thrown by the Earth is bright, but the rest of the Moon is always seen to be dark. From which circumstance we understand without hesitation that this brightness is due to the proximity of the Sun's rays coming into contact with some denser region which surrounds the Moon as an envelope; owing to which contact a sort of dawn-light is diffused over the neighbouring regions of the Moon, just as the twilight spreads in the morning and evening on the Earth;[1] but I will

---

[1] The illumination of the Moon in eclipses, noticed by Galileo, is now referred to the refraction of the sunlight by the earth's atmosphere, and the reddish colour of the light is explained by Herschel (*Outlines of*

C

treat more fully of this matter in my book upon the *System of the Universe.*[1]

Again, to assert that this sort of light is imparted to the Moon by the planet Venus is so childish as to be undeserving of an answer; for who is so ignorant as not to understand that at conjunction and within an angular distance of 60° it is quite impossible for the part of the Moon turned away from the Sun to be seen by the planet Venus?

But that this light is derived from the Sun penetrating with its light the solid mass of the Moon, and rendering it luminous, is equally untenable. For then this light would never lessen, since the hemisphere of the Moon is always illumined by the Sun, except at the moment of a lunar eclipse, yet really it quickly decreases while the Moon is drawing near to the end of her first quarter, and when she has passed.

Astronomy, ch. vii.) to be due to the absorption of the violet and blue rays by the aqueous vapour of the Earth's atmosphere. The idea of a sensible lunar atmosphere is not in accordance with the observed phenomena of the occultations of stars.

[1] Galileo's *Systema Mundi.* Owing to the violent opposition provoked by the discussion of the discoveries of Galileo, and their bearing on the Copernican system of astronomy, Galileo seems to have found it necessary to delay the publication of this work until 1632, when, believing himself safe under the friendship and patronage of Pope Urban VIII. and others in power at Rome, he at length published it. Urban, however, now turned against him, denounced the book and its author, and summoned him to Rome, where the well-known incidents of his trial and condemnation took place.

her first quarter it becomes quite dull. Since, therefore, this kind of secondary brightness is not inherent
and the Moon's own, nor borrowed from any of the
stars, nor from the Sun, and since there now remains
in the whole universe no other body whatever except
the Earth, what, pray, must we conclude? What must
we assert? Shall we assert that the body of the
Moon, or some other dark and sunless orb, receives
light from the Earth? Why should it not be the
Moon? And most certainly it is. The Earth, with
fair and grateful exchange, pays back to the Moon an
illumination like that which it receives from the
Moon nearly the whole time during the darkest
gloom of night. Let me explain the matter more
clearly. At conjunction, when the Moon occupies
a position between the Sun and the Earth, the
Moon is illuminated by the Sun's rays on her half
towards the Sun which is turned away from the Earth,
and the other half, with which she regards the Earth,
is covered with darkness, and so in no degree illumines
the Earth's surface. When the Moon has slightly
separated from the Sun, straightway she is partly
illumined on the half directed towards us; she turns
towards us a slender silvery crescent, and slightly
illumines the Earth; the Sun's illumination increases
upon the Moon as she approaches her first quarter,

and the reflexion of that light increases on the Earth; the brightness in the Moon next extends beyond the semicircle, and our nights grow brighter; at length the entire face of the Moon looking towards the Earth is irradiated with the most intense brightness by the Sun, which happens when the Sun and Moon are on opposite sides of the Earth; then far and wide the surface of the Earth shines with the flood of moon-light; after this the Moon, now waning, sends out less powerful beams, and the Earth is illumined less powerfully; at length the Moon draws near her first position of conjunction with the Sun, and forthwith black night invades the Earth. In such a cycle the moonlight gives us each month alternations of brighter and fainter illumination. But the benefit of her light to the Earth is balanced and repaid by the benefit of the light of the Earth to her; for while the Moon is found near the Sun about the time of conjunction, she has in front of her the entire surface of that hemi-sphere of the Earth which is exposed to the Sun, and vividly illumined with his beams, and so receives light reflected from the Earth. Owing to such re-flexion, the hemisphere of the Moon nearer to us, though deprived of sunlight, appears of considerable brightness. Again, when removed from the Sun through a quadrant, the Moon sees only one-half of

the Earth's hemisphere illuminated, namely the
western half, for the other, the eastern, is covered
with the shades of night; the Moon is, therefore, less
brightly enlightened by the Earth, and accordingly
that secondary light appears fainter to us. But if
you imagine the Moon to be set on the opposite side
of the Earth to the Sun, she will see the hemisphere
of the Earth, now between the Moon and the Sun,
quite dark, and steeped in the gloom of night; if,
therefore, an eclipse should accompany such a position of the Moon, she will receive no light at all, being
deprived of the illumination of the Sun and Earth
together. In any other position, with regard to the
Earth and the Sun, the Moon receives more or less
light by reflexion from the Earth, according as she
sees a greater or smaller portion of the hemisphere of
the Earth illuminated by the Sun; for such a law is
observed between these two orbs, that at whatever
times the Earth is most brightly enlightened by the
Moon, at those times, on the contrary, the Moon is
least enlightened by the Earth; and contrariwise.
Let these few words on this subject suffice in this
place; for I will consider it more fully in my *System
of the Universe*, where, by very many arguments and
experimental proofs, there is shown to be a very
strong reflexion of the Sun's light from the Earth, for

the benefit of those who urge that the Earth must
be separated from the starry host, chiefly for the
reason that it has neither motion nor light, for I will
prove that the Earth has motion, and surpasses the
Moon in brightness, and is not the place where the
dull refuse of the universe has settled down; and I
will support my demonstration by a thousand arguments taken from natural phenomena.

Stars. Their appearance in the telescope.

Hitherto I have spoken of the observations which I
have made concerning the Moon's body; now I will
briefly announce the phenomena which have been,
as yet, seen by me with reference to the Fixed Stars.
And first of all the following fact is worthy of consideration :—The stars, fixed as well as erratic, when
seen with a telescope, by no means appear to be
increased in magnitude in the same proportion as
other objects, and the Moon herself, gain increase of
size ; but in the case of the stars such increase appears
much less, so that you may consider that a telescope,
which (for the sake of illustration) is powerful enough
to magnify other objects a hundred times, will scarcely
render the stars magnified four or five times.   But
the reason of this is as follows :—When stars are
viewed with our natural eyesight they do not present
themselves to us of their bare, real size, but beaming
with a certain vividness, and fringed with sparkling

.rays, especially when the night is far advanced; and from this circumstance they appear much larger than they would if they were stripped of those adventitious fringes, for the angle which they subtend at the eye is determined not by the primary disc of the star, but, by the brightness which so widely surrounds it. Perhaps you will understand this most clearly from the well-known circumstance that when stars rise just at sunset, in the beginning of twilight, they appear very small, although they may be stars of the first magnitude; and even the planet Venus itself, on any occasion when it may present itself to view in broad daylight, is so small to see that it scarcely seems to equal a star of the last magnitude. It is different in the case of other objects, and even of the Moon, which, whether viewed in the light of midday or in the depth of night, always appears of the same size. We conclude therefore that the stars are seen at midnight in uncurtailed glory, but their fringes are of such a nature that the daylight can cut them off, and not only daylight, but any slight cloud which may be interposed between a star and the eye of the observer. A dark veil or coloured glass has the same effect, for, upon placing them before the eye between it and the stars, all the blaze that surrounds them leaves them at once. A telescope also accomplishes

the same result, for it removes from the stars their
adventitious and accidental splendours before it
enlarges their true discs (if indeed they are of that
shape), and so they seem less magnified than other
objects, for a star of the fifth or sixth magnitude seen
through a telescope is shown as of the first magnitude
only.

The difference between the appearance of the
planets and the fixed stars seems also deserving of
notice. The planets present their discs perfectly
round, just as if described with a pair of compasses,
and appear as so many little moons, completely illuminated and of a globular shape; but the fixed stars
do not look to the naked eye bounded by a circular
circumference, but rather like blazes of light, shooting
out beams on all sides and very sparkling, and with a
telescope they appear of the same shape as when they
are viewed by simply looking at them, but so much
larger that a star of the fifth or sixth magnitude
seems to equal Sirius, the largest of all the fixed stars.[1]

Telescopic
Stars: their
infinite

But beyond the stars of the sixth magnitude you
will behold through the telescope a host of other stars,

---

[1] The immense distance of stars makes it impossible for them to be
magnified by any telescope, however powerful; the apparent or spurious
disc is an optical effect, which depends on the telescope used, and is
smallest with the largest aperture.

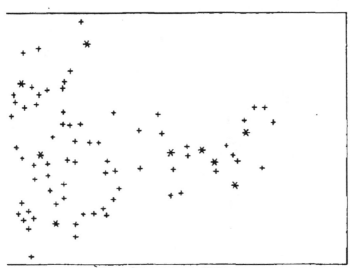

Orion's Belt and Sword; 83 Stars

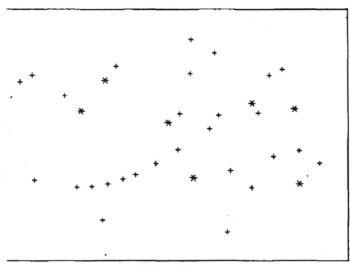

Pleiades; 36 Stars

ɔ:"Sidereus Nuncius."

which escape the unassisted sight, so numerous as to multitude. As examples, Orion's Belt and Sword and the Pleiades are described as seen by Galileo.
be almost beyond belief, for you may see more than
six other differences of magnitude, and the largest of
these, which I may call stars of the seventh magnitude, or of the first magnitude of invisible stars, appear with the aid of the telescope larger and brighter
than stars of the second magnitude seen with the
unassisted sight. But in order that you may see one
or two proofs of the inconceivable manner in which
they are crowded together, I have determined to
make out a case against two star-clusters, that from
them as a specimen you may decide about the rest.

As my first example I had determined to depict
the entire constellation of Orion, but I was over-
whelmed by the vast quantity of stars and by want
of time, and so I have deferred attempting this to
another occasion, for there are adjacent to, or scattered
among, the old stars more than five hundred new
stars within the limits of one or two degrees. For
this reason I have selected the three stars in Orion's
Belt and the six in his Sword, which have been long
well-known groups, and I have added eighty other
stars recently discovered in their vicinity, and I have
preserved as exactly as possible the intervals between
them. The well-known or old stars, for the sake of
distinction, I have depicted of larger size, and I have

outlined them with a double line; the others, invisible to the naked eye, I have marked smaller and with one line only. I have also preserved the differences of magnitude as much as I could.

As a second example I have depicted the six stars of the constellation Taurus, called the Pleiades (I say *six* intentionally, since the seventh is scarcely ever visible), a group of stars which is enclosed in the heavens within very narrow precincts. Near these there lie more than forty others invisible to the naked eye, no one of which is much more than half a degree off any of the aforesaid six; of these I have noticed only thirty-six in my diagram. I have preserved their intervals, magnitudes, and the distinction between the old and the new stars, just as in the case of the constellation Orion.

The Milky Way consists entirely of stars in countless numbers and of various magnitudes.

The next object which I have observed is the essence or substance of the Milky Way. By the aid of a telescope any one may behold this in a manner which so distinctly appeals to the senses that all the disputes which have tormented philosophers through so many ages are exploded at once by the irrefragable evidence of our eyes, and we are freed from wordy disputes upon this subject, for the Galaxy is nothing else but a mass of innumerable stars planted together in clusters. Upon whatever part of it you direct the

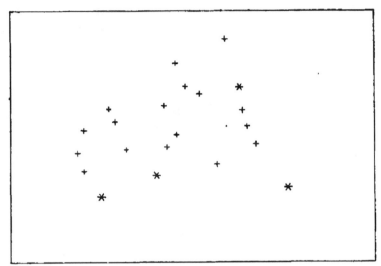

Star-cluster in Orion's Head

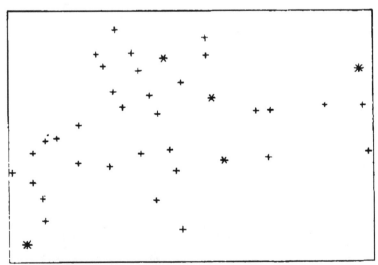

Star-cluster of Praesepe in Cancer

Galileo: "Sidereus Nuncius", Venice, 1610.

telescope straightway a vast crowd of stars presents itself to view; many of them are tolerably large and extremely bright, but the number of small ones is quite beyond determination.

And whereas that milky brightness, like the brightness of a white cloud, is not only to be seen in the Milky Way, but several spots of a similar colour shine faintly here and there in the heavens, if you turn the telescope upon any of them you will find a cluster of stars packed close together. Further—and you will be more surprised at this,—the stars which have been called by every one of the astronomers up to this day *nebulous*, are groups of small stars set thick together in a wonderful way, and although each one of them on account of its smallness, or its immense distance from us, escapes our sight, from the commingling of their rays there arises that brightness which has hitherto been believed to be the denser part of the heavens, able to reflect the rays of the stars or the Sun.

I have observed some of these, and I wish to subjoin the star-clusters of two of these nebulæ. First, you have a diagram of the nebula called that of Orion's Head, in which I have counted twenty-one stars.

The second cluster contains the nebula called Præsepe, which is not one star only, but a mass of more

Side note: Nebulæ resolved into clusters of stars: as examples, the nebula in Orion's Head and Præsepe.

than forty small stars. I have noticed thirty-six stars, besides the Aselli, arranged in the order of the accompanying diagram.

Discovery of Jupiter's satellites, Jan. 7, 1610: record of Galileo's observations during two months. I have now finished my brief account of the observations which I have thus far made with regard to the Moon, the Fixed Stars, and the Galaxy. There remains the matter, which seems to me to deserve to be considered the most important in this work, namely, that I should disclose and publish to the world the occasion of discovering and observing four PLANETS, never seen from the very beginning of the world up to our own times, their positions, and the observations made during the last two months about their movements and their changes of magnitude; and I summon all astronomers to apply themselves to examine and determine their periodic times, which it has not been permitted me to achieve up to this day, owing to the restriction of my time. I give them warning however again, so that they may not approach such an inquiry to no purpose, that they will want a very accurate telescope, and such as I have described in the beginning of this account.

On the 7th day of January in the present year, 1610, in the first[1] hour of the following night, when I

---

[1] The times of Galileo's observations are to be understood as reckoned from sunset.

was viewing the constellations of the heavens through a telescope, the planet Jupiter presented itself to my view, and as I had prepared for myself a very excellent instrument, I noticed a circumstance which I had never been able to notice before, owing to want of power in my other telescope, namely, that three little stars, small but very bright, were near the planet; and although I believed them to belong to the number of the fixed stars, yet they made me somewhat wonder, because they seemed to be arranged exactly in a straight line, parallel to the ecliptic,[1] and to be brighter than the rest of the stars, equal to them in magnitude. The position of them with reference to one another and to Jupiter was as follows (Fig. 1).

On the east side there were two stars, and a single one towards the west. The star which was furthest towards the east, and the western star, appeared rather larger than the third.

I scarcely troubled at all about the distance between them and Jupiter, for, as I have already said, at first I believed them to be fixed stars; but when on January 8th, led by some fatality, I turned again to look

---

[1] The satellites of Jupiter revolve in planes very nearly, although not exactly, coincident with that of the equator of the planet, which is inclined 3° 5' 30" to the orbit of the planet, and the plane of the orbit is inclined 1° 18' 51" to the ecliptic.

at the same part of the heavens, I found a very different state of things, for there were three little stars all west of Jupiter, and nearer together than on the previous night, and they were separated from one another by equal intervals, as the accompanying illustration (Fig. 2) shows.

At this point, although I had not turned my thoughts at all upon the approximation of the stars to one another, yet my surprise began to be excited, how Jupiter could one day be found to the east of all the aforesaid fixed stars when the day before it had been west of two of them; and forthwith I became afraid lest the planet might have moved differently from the calculation of astronomers, and so had passed those stars by its own proper motion. I therefore waited for the next night with the most intense longing, but I was disappointed of my hope, for the sky was covered with clouds in every direction.

But on January 10th the stars appeared in the following position with regard to Jupiter; there were two only, and both on the east side of Jupiter, the third, as I thought, being hidden by the planet (Fig. 3). They were situated just as before, exactly in the same straight line with Jupiter, and along the Zodiac.

When I had seen these phenomena, as I knew that

corresponding changes of position could not by any
means belong to Jupiter, and as, moreover, I perceived
that the stars which I saw had been always the same,
for there were no others either in front or behind,
within a great distance, along the Zodiac,—at length,
changing from doubt into surprise, I discovered that
the interchange of position which I saw belonged not
to Jupiter, but to the stars to which my attention had
been drawn, and I thought therefore that they ought
to be observed henceforward with more attention
and precision.

Accordingly, on January 11th I saw an arrangement of the following kind (Fig. 4), namely, only
two stars to the east of Jupiter, the nearer of which
was distant from Jupiter three times as far as from
the star further to the east; and the star furthest to
the east was nearly twice as large as the other one;
whereas on the previous night they had appeared
nearly of equal magnitude. I therefore concluded,
and decided unhesitatingly, that there are three stars
in the heavens moving about Jupiter, as Venus and
Mercury round the Sun; which at length was estab-
lished as clear as daylight by numerous other subse-
quent observations. These observations also estab-
lished that there are not only three, but four, erratic
sidereal bodies performing their revolutions round

Jupiter, observations of whose changes of position made with more exactness on succeeding nights the following account will supply. I have measured also the intervals between them with the telescope in the manner already explained. Besides this, I have given the times of observation, especially when several were made in the same night, for the revolutions of these planets are so swift that an observer may generally get differences of position every hour.

Jan. 12.—At the first hour of the next night I saw these heavenly bodies arranged in this manner (Fig. 5). The satellite[1] furthest to the east was greater than the satellite furthest to the west; but both were very conspicuous and bright; the distance of each one from Jupiter was two minutes. A third satellite, certainly not in view before, began to appear at the third hour; it nearly touched Jupiter on the east side, and was exceedingly small. They were all arranged in the same straight line, along the ecliptic.

Jan. 13.—For the first time four satellites were in view in the following position with regard to Jupiter (Fig. 6).

---

[1] Galileo continues to call these bodies *stars*, perhaps meaning "Medicean stars," throughout the description of their configurations, but as he had now detected their nature, it is more convenient to call them *satellites*, the term introduced by Kepler.

There were three to the west, and one to the east; they made a straight line nearly, but the middle satellite of those to the west deviated a little from the straight line towards the north. The satellite furthest to the east was at a distance of 2′ from Jupiter; there were intervals of 1′ only between Jupiter and the nearest satellite, and between the satellites themselves, west of Jupiter. All the satellites appeared of the same size, and though small they were very brilliant, and far outshone the fixed stars of the same magnitude.

Jan. 14.—The weather was cloudy.

Jan. 15.—At the third hour of the night the four satellites were in the state depicted in the next diagram (Fig. 7) with reference to Jupiter.

All were to the west, and arranged nearly in the same straight line; but the satellite which counted third from Jupiter was raised a little to the north. The nearest to Jupiter was the smallest of all; the rest appeared larger and in order of magnitude; the intervals between Jupiter and the three nearest satellites were all equal, and were of the magnitude of 2′ each; but the satellite furthest to the west was distant 4′ from the satellite nearest to it. They were very brilliant, and not at all twinkling, as they have always appeared both before and since. But at the seventh hour there were only three satellites, presenting with Jupiter an appearance of the following kind (Fig. 8). They were, that is to say, in the same straight line to a hair;. the nearest to Jupiter was very small, and distant from the planet 3′; the distance of the second from this one was 1′; and of the third from the second 4′ 30″. But after another hour the two middle satellites were still nearer, for they were only 30″, or less, apart.

Jan. 16.—At the first hour of the night I saw three satellites arranged in this order (Fig. 9). Jupiter was between two of them, which were at a distance of 0′ 40″ from the planet on either side, and the third was west of Jupiter at a distance of 8′. The satellites near to Jupiter appeared brighter than the satellite further off, but not larger.

Jan. 17, after sunset 0 hours 30 minutes, the configuration was of this kind (Fig. 10). There was one satellite only to the east, at. a distance of 3′ from Jupiter; to the west likewise there was only one satellite, distant 11′ from Jupiter. The satellite on the east appeared twice as large as the satellite to the west; and there were no more than these two. But four hours after, that is, nearly at the fifth hour, a third satellite began to emerge on the east side, which, before its appearance, as I think, had been joined with the former of the two other satellites, and the position was of this kind (Fig. 11). The middle satellite was very near indeed to the satellite on the east, and was only 20″ from it; and was a little towards the south of the straight line drawn through the two extreme satellites and Jupiter.

Jan. 18, at 0 h. 20 m. after sunset, the appearance was such as this (Fig. 12). The satellite to the east was larger than the western one, and was at a distance from Jupiter of 8′, the western one being at a distance of 10′.

Jan. 19.—At the second hour of the night the relative position of the satellites was such as this (Fig. 13); that is, there were three satellites exactly in a straight line with Jupiter, one to the east, at a distance of 6′ from Jupiter; between Jupiter and the first satellite to the west in order, there was an interval of 5′; this satellite was 4′ off the other one more to the west. At that time I was doubtful whether or no there was a satellite between the satellite to the east and Jupiter, but so very close to Jupiter as almost to touch the planet; but at the fifth hour I saw this satellite distinctly, by that time occupying exactly the middle position between Jupiter and the eastern satellite, so that the configuration was thus (Fig. 14). Moreover, the satellite which had just come into view was very small; yet at the sixth hour it was nearly as large as the rest.

Jan. 20 : 1 h. 15 m.—A similar arrangement was seen (Fig. 15). There were three satellites, so small as scarcely to be distinguishable ; their distances from Jupiter, and from one another, were not more than 1′. I was doubtful whether on the western side there were two satellites or three. About the sixth hour they were grouped in this way (Fig. 16). The eastern satellite was twice as far away from Jupiter as before, that is 2′; on the western side, the satellite in the middle was distant from Jupiter 0′ 40″, and from the satellite still further to the west 0′ 20″; at length, at the seventh hour, three satellites were seen on the western side (Fig. 17). The satellite nearest to Jupiter was distant from the planet 0′ 20″; between this one and the satellite furthest to the west there was an interval of 40″, but between these another satellite was in view slightly southward of them, and not more than 10″ off the most westerly satellite.

Jan. 21 : 0 h. 30 m.—There were three satellites on the east side ; the satellites and Jupiter were at equal distances apart (Fig. 18). The intervals were by estimation 50″ each. There was also one satellite on the west, distant 4′ from Jupiter. The satellite on the east side nearest to Jupiter was the least of all.

Jan. 22 : 2 h.—The grouping of the satellites was similar (Fig. 19). There was an interval of 5′ from the satellite on the east to Jupiter; from Jupiter to the satellite furthest to the west 7′. The two interior satellites on the western side were 0′ 40″ apart, and the satellite nearer to Jupiter was 1′ from the planet. The inner satellites were smaller than the outer ones, but they were situated all in the same straight line, along the ecliptic, except that the middle of the three western satellites was slightly to the south of it, but at the sixth hour of the night they appeared in this position (Fig. 20). The satellite on the east was very small, at a distance from Jupiter of 5′ as before ; but the three satellites on the west were separated by equal distances from Jupiter and from each other; and the intervals were nearly 1′ 20″ each. The satellite nearest Jupiter appeared smaller than the other two on the same side, but they all appeared arranged exactly in the same straight line.

Jan. 23, at 0 h. 40 m. after sunset, the grouping of the satellites was nearly after this fashion (Fig. 21). There were three satellites with Jupiter in a straight line along the ecliptic, as they always have been; two were on the east of the planet, one on the west; the satellite furthest to the east was 7′ from the next one, and this satellite 2′ 40″ from Jupiter; Jupiter was 3′ 20″ from the satellite on the west; and they were all of nearly the same size. But at the fifth hour the two satellites which had been previously near Jupiter were no longer visible, being, as I suppose, hidden behind Jupiter, and the appearance presented was such as this (Fig. 22).

Jan. 24.—Three satellites, all on the east side, were visible, and nearly, but not quite, in the same straight line with Jupiter, for the satellite in the middle was slightly to. the south of it (Fig. 23). The satellite nearest to Jupiter was 2′ distant from the planet; the next in order 0′ 30″ from this satellite, and the third was 9′ further off still; they were all very bright. But at the sixth hour two satellites only presented themselves to view in this position, namely in the same straight line with Jupiter exactly, and the distance of the nearest to the planet was lengthened to 3′; the next was 2′ further off, and unless I am mistaken, the two satellites previously observed in the middle had come together, and appeared as one.

Jan. 25, at 1 h. 40 m., the satellites were grouped thus (Fig. 24). There were only two satellites on the east side, and these were rather large. The satellite furthest to the east was 5′ from the satellite in the middle, and it was 6′ from Jupiter.

Jan. 26, at 0 h. 40 m., the relative positions of the satellites were thus (Fig. 25). Three satellites

were in view, of which two were east and the
third west of Jupiter; this one was distant 3′ from
the planet. On the east side the satellite in the
middle was at a distance of 5′ 20″; the further satellite was 6′ beyond; they were arranged in a straight
line, and were of the same size. At the fifth hour the
arrangement was nearly the same, with this difference
only, that the fourth satellite was emerging on the east
side near Jupiter. It was smaller than the rest, and
was then at a distance of 0′ 30″ from Jupiter; but
was raised a little above the straight line towards the
north, as the accompanying figure shows (Fig. 26).

Jan. 27, 1 h. after sunset, a single satellite only
was in view, and that on the east side of Jupiter in
this position (Fig. 27). It was very small, and at a
distance of 7′ from Jupiter.

Jan. 28 and 29.—Owing to the intervention of
clouds, I could make no observation.

Jan. 30.—At the first hour of the night the satellites were in view, arranged in the following way
(Fig. 28). There was one satellite on the east side, at
a distance of 2′ 30″ from Jupiter; and there were two
satellites on the west, of which the one nearer to
Jupiter was 3′ off the planet, and the other satellite 1′
further. The places of the outer satellites and Jupiter
were in the same straight line; but the satellite in

the middle was a little above it to the north. The satellite furthest to the west was smaller than the rest.

On the last day of the month, at the second hour, two satellites on the east side were visible, and one on the west (Fig. 29). Of the satellites east of the planet, the one in the middle was 2′ 20″ distant from Jupiter; and the satellite further to the east was 0′ 30″ from the middle satellite; the satellite on the west was at a distance of 1′0′ from Jupiter. They were in the same straight line nearly, and would have been exactly so, only the satellite on the east nearest to Jupiter was raised a little towards the north. At the fourth hour, the two satellites on the east were still nearer together, for they were only 20″ apart (Fig. 30). The western satellite appeared rather small in these two observations.

Feb. 1.—At the second hour of the night the arrangement was similar (Fig. 31). The satellite furthest to the east was at a distance of 6′ from Jupiter, and the western satellite 8′. On the east side there was a very small satellite, at a distance of 20″ from Jupiter. They made a perfectly straight line.

Feb. 2.—The satellites were seen arranged thus (Fig. 32). There was one only on the east, at a dis-

tance of 6′ from Jupiter. Jupiter was 4′ from the
nearest satellite on the west; between this satellite
and the satellite further to the west there was an
interval of 8′; they were in the same straight line
exactly, and were nearly of the same magnitude.
But at the seventh hour four satellites were there
—two on each side of Jupiter (Fig. 33). Of
these satellites, the most easterly was at a distance
of 4′ from the next; this satellite was 1′ 40″ from
Jupiter; Jupiter was 6′ from the nearest satellite on
the west, and this one from the satellite further to
the west, 8′; and they were all alike in the same
straight line, drawn in the direction of the Zodiac.

Feb. 3 : 7 h.—The satellites were arranged in the
following way (Fig. 34):—The satellite on the east
was at a distance of 1′ 30″ from Jupiter; the nearest
satellite on the west, 2′, and there was a long distance, 10′, from this satellite to the satellite further
to the west. They were exactly in the same straight
line, and of equal magnitude.

Feb. 4 : 2 h.—Four satellites attended Jupiter, two
on the east and two on the west, arranged in one perfectly straight line, as in the adjoining figure (Fig. 35).
The satellite furthest to the east was at a distance of
3′ from the next satellite. This one was 0′ 40″ from
Jupiter; Jupiter 4′ from the nearest satellite on the

west ; and this one from the satellite further to the west 6'. In magnitude they were nearly equal ; the satellite nearest to Jupiter was rather smaller in appearance than the rest. But at the seventh hour (Fig. 36) the eastern satellites were at a distance of only 0' 30" apart. Jupiter was 2' from the nearest satellite on the east ; and from the satellite on the west, next in order, 4' ; this one was distant 3' from the satellite further to the west. They were all equal in magnitude, and in a straight line, drawn in the direction of the ecliptic.

Feb. 5.—The sky was cloudy.

Feb. 6.—Two satellites only appeared, with Jupiter between them, as is seen in the accompanying figure (Fig. 37). The satellite on the east was 2' from Jupiter, and that on the west 3'. They were in the same straight line with Jupiter, and were equal in magnitude.

Feb. 7.—There were two satellites by the side of Jupiter, and both of them on the east of the planet, arranged in this manner (Fig. 38). The intervals between the satellites and Jupiter were equal, and of 1' each ; and a straight line would go through them and the centre of Jupiter.

Feb. 8 : 1 h.—Three satellites were there, all on the east side of Jupiter, as in the diagram (Fig. 39).

The nearest to Jupiter, a rather small one, was distant from the planet 1′ 20″; the middle one was 4′ from this satellite, and was rather large; the satellite furthest to the east, a very small one, was at a distance of 0′ 20″ from this satellite. It was doubtful whether there was one satellite near to Jupiter or two, for sometimes it seemed that there was another satellite by its side towards the east, wonderfully small, and only 10″ from it. They were all situated at points in a straight line drawn in the direction of the Zodiac. At the third hour the satellite nearest to Jupiter was almost touching the planet, for it was only distant 10″ from it; but the others had become further off, for the middle one was 6′ from Jupiter. At length, at the fourth hour, the satellite which was previously the nearest to Jupiter joined with the planet and disappeared.

Feb. 9 : 0 h. 30 m.—There were two satellites on the east side of Jupiter, and one on the west, in an arrangement such as this (Fig. 40). The satellite furthest to the east, which was a rather small one, was distant 4′ from the next satellite; the satellite in the middle was larger, and at a distance of 7′ from Jupiter. Jupiter was distant 4′ from the western satellite, which was a small one.

Feb. 10 : 1 h. 30 m.—A pair of satellites, very small, and both on the east of the planet, were visible, in the following position (Fig. 41). The further satellite was distant from Jupiter 10′, the nearer 0′ 20″, and they were in the same straight line ; but at the fourth hour the satellite nearest to Jupiter no longer appeared, and the other seemed so diminished that it could scarcely be kept in sight, although the atmosphere was quite clear, and the satellite was further from Jupiter than before, since its distance was now 12′.

Feb. 11 : 1 h.—There were two satellites on the east, and one on the west (Fig. 42). The western satellite was at a distance of 4′ from Jupiter. The satellite on the east, nearest to the planet, was likewise 4′ from Jupiter ; but the satellite further to the east was at a distance from this one of 8′ ; they were fairly clear to view, and in the same straight line ; but at the third hour the fourth satellite was visible near to Jupiter on the east, less in magnitude than the rest, separated from Jupiter by a distance of 0′ 30″, and slightly to the north out of the straight line drawn through the rest (Fig. 43). They were all very bright and extremely distinct, but at 5 h. 30 m. the satellite on the east nearest to Jupiter had moved further away from the planet, and was occupying a position midway between the planet and the neighbouring satellite further to the east. They were all in the same straight line exactly, and of the same magnitude, as may be seen in the accompanying diagram (Fig. 44).

Feb. 12 : 0 h. 40 m.—A pair of satellites on the east, a pair likewise on the west, were near the planet (Fig. 45). The satellite on the east furthest removed from Jupiter was at a distance of 10′, and the further of the satellites on the west was 8′ off. They were both fairly distinct. The other two were very near to Jupiter, and very small, especially the satellite to the east, which was at a distance of 0′ 40″ from Jupiter. The distance of the western satellite was 1′. But at the fourth hour the satellite which was nearest to Jupiter on the east was visible no longer.

Feb. 13 : 0 h. 30 m.—Two satellites were visible in the east, two also in the west (Fig. 46). The satellite on the east near Jupiter was fairly distinct ; its distance from the planet was 2′. The satellite further to the east was less noticeable ; it was distant 4′ from the other. Of the satellites on the west, the one furthest from Jupiter, which was very distinct, was parted from the planet 4′. Between this satellite and Jupiter intervened a small satellite close to the most westerly satellite, being not more than 0′ 3″ off. They were all in the same straight line, corresponding exactly to the direction of the ecliptic.

Feb. 15 (for on the 14th the sky was covered with clouds), at the first hour, the position of the satellites was thus (Fig. 47) ; that is, there were three satellites on the east, but none were visible on the west. The satellite on the east nearest to Jupiter was at a distance of 0′ 50″ from the planet ; the next in order was 0′ 20″ from this satellite, and the furthest to the east was 2′ from the second satellite, and it was larger than the others, for those nearer to Jupiter were very small. But about the fifth hour only one of the satellites which had been near to Jupiter was to be seen ; its distance from Jupiter was 0′ 30″. The distance of the satellite furthest to the east from Jupiter had increased, for it was then 4′ (Fig. 48). But at the sixth hour, besides the two situated as just described on the east, one satellite was visible towards the west, very small, at a distance of 2′ from Jupiter (Fig. 49).

Feb. 16 : 6 h.—Their places were arranged as follows (Fig. 50) ; that is, the satellite on the east was 7′ from Jupiter, Jupiter 5′ from the next satellite on the west, and this 3′ from the remaining satellite still further to the west. They were all of the same magnitude nearly, rather bright, and in the same straight line, corresponding accurately to the direction of the Zodiac.

Feb. 17 : 1 h.—Two satellites were in view, one on

the east, distant 3' from Jupiter ; the other on the west, distant 10' (Fig. 51). The latter was somewhat less than the satellite on the east ; but at the sixth hour the eastern satellite was nearer to Jupiter, being at a distance of 0' 50", and the western satellite was further off, namely 12'. At both observations they were in the same straight line with Jupiter, and were both rather small, especially the eastern satellite in the second observation.

Feb. 18 : 1 h.—Three satellites were in view, of which two were on the west and one on the east ; the distance of the eastern satellite from Jupiter was 3', and of the nearest satellite on the west 2' ; the remaining satellite, still further to the west, was 8' from the middle satellite (Fig. 52). They were all in the same straight line exactly, and of about the same magnitude. But at the second hour the satellites nearest to the planet were at equal distances from Jupiter, for the western satellite was now also 3' from the planet. But at the sixth hour the fourth satellite was visible between the satellite on the east and Jupiter, in the following configuration (Fig. 53). The satellite furthest to the east was at a distance of 3' from the next in order ; this one was at a distance of 1' 50" from Jupiter ; Jupiter was at a distance of 3' from the next satellite on the west, and this 7' from the satellite still further to the west. These were nearly equal in magnitude, only the satellite on the east nearest to Jupiter was a little smaller than the rest, and they were all in the same straight line parallel to the ecliptic.

Feb. 19 : 0 h. 40 m.—Two satellites only were in view, west of Jupiter, rather large, and arranged exactly in the same straight line with Jupiter, in the direction of the ecliptic (Fig. 54). The nearer satellite was at a distance of 7′ from Jupiter and of 6′ from the satellite further to the west.

Feb. 20.—The sky was cloudy.

Feb. 21 : 1 h. 30 m.—Three satellites, rather small, were in view, placed thus (Fig. 55). The satellite to the east was 2′ from Jupiter; Jupiter was 3′ from the next, which was on the west; and this one was 7′ from the satellite further to the west. They were exactly in the same straight line parallel to the ecliptic.

Feb. 25 : 1 h. 30 m. (for on the three previous nights the sky was overcast).—Three satellites appeared, two on the east, which were at a distance of 4′ apart, the same as the distance of the nearer satellite from Jupiter; on the west there was one satellite at a distance of 2′ from Jupiter. They were exactly in the same straight line in the direction of the ecliptic (Fig. 56).

Feb. 26 : 0 h. 30 m.—A pair of satellites only

were present, one on the east, distant 10′ from Jupiter; the other was on the west, at a distance of 6′ (Fig. 57). The eastern satellite was slightly smaller than the western. At the fifth hour three satellites were visible; for, besides the two already noticed, a third satellite was in view, on the west, near Jupiter, very small, which previously had been hidden behind Jupiter, and it was at a distance of 1′ from the planet (Fig. 58).

But the satellite on the east was seen to be further off than before, being at a distance of 11′ from Jupiter. On this night, for the first time, I determined to observe the motion of Jupiter and the adjacent planets (his satellites) along the zodiac, by reference to some fixed star; for there was a fixed star in view, eastwards of Jupiter, at a distance of 11′ from the satellite on the east, and a little to the south, in the following manner (Fig. 59).

· Feb. 27: 1h. 4 m.—The satellites appeared in the following configuration. The satellite furthest to the east was at a distance of 10′ from Jupiter; the next in order was near Jupiter, being at a distance of 0′ 30″ from the planet. The next satellite was on the western side, at a distance of 2′ 30″ from Jupiter; and the satellite further to the west was at a distance of 1′ from this. The two satellites near to Jupiter

E

appeared small, especially the satellite on the east;
but the satellites furthest off were very bright, particularly that on the west, and they made a straight
line in the direction of the ecliptic exactly. The
motion of the planets towards the east was plainly
seen by reference to the aforesaid fixed star, for Jupiter
and his attendant satellites were nearer to it, as may
be seen in the accompanying figure (Fig. 60). At the
fifth hour the satellite on the east, near to Jupiter,
was 1' from the planet.

Feb. 28 : 1 h.—Only two satellites were visible, one
on the east, at a distance of 9' from Jupiter, and
another on the west, at a distance of 2'; they were
both rather bright, and in the same straight line with
Jupiter, and a straight line drawn from the fixed
star perpendicular to this straight line fell upon the
satellite on the east, as in the figure (Fig. 61). At
the fifth hour a third satellite was seen at a distance
of 2' from Jupiter, on the east, in the position shown
in the figure (Fig. 62).

March 1 : 0 h. 40 m.—Four satellites, all on the
east of the planet, were seen; the satellite nearest to
Jupiter was 2' from the planet; the next 1' from
this; the third was 0' 20" from the second, and was
brighter than the others; and the satellite still further
to the east was at a distance of 4' from it, and was

smaller than the others (Fig. 63). They made a
straight line very nearly, only the satellite third from
Jupiter was slightly above the line. The fixed star
formed with Jupiter and the most easterly satellite
an equilateral triangle, as in the figure.

March 2: 0 h. 40 m.—Three satellites were in
attendance, two on the east and one on the west, in
the configuration shown in the diagram (Fig. 64).
The satellite furthest to the east was 7′ from
Jupiter; from this satellite the next was distant 0′ 30″,
and the satellite on the west was separated from
Jupiter by an interval of 2′. The satellites furthest
off were brighter and larger than the remaining
satellite, which appeared very small. The satellite
furthest to the east seemed to be raised a little
towards the north, out of the straight line drawn
through the other satellites and Jupiter.

The fixed star already noticed was at a distance of
8′ from the western satellite, that is, from the perpendicular drawn from that satellite to the straight
line drawn through all the system, as shown in the
figure given.

These determinations of the motion of Jupiter and
the adjacent planets (his satellites) by reference to a
fixed star, I have thought well to present to the
notice of astronomers, in order that any one may be

able to understand from them that the movements
of these planets (Jupiter's satellites) both in longitude
and in latitude agree exactly with the motions [of
Jupiter] which are extracted from tables.

These are my observations upon the four Medicean
planets, recently discovered for the first time by me;
and although it is not yet permitted me to deduce by
calculation from these observations the orbits of these
bodies, yet I may be allowed to make some statements, based upon them, well worthy of attention.

Deductions
from the
previous
observations
concerning
the orbits
and periods
of Jupiter's
satellites.

And, in the first place, since they are sometimes
behind, sometimes before Jupiter, at like distances,
and withdraw from this planet towards the east and
towards the west only within very narrow limits
of divergence, and since they accompany this planet
alike when its motion is retrograde and direct, it can
be a matter of doubt to no one that they perform
their revolutions about this planet, while at the same
time they all accomplish together orbits of twelve
years' length about the centre of the world. Moreover, they revolve in unequal circles, which is evidently the conclusion to be drawn from the fact that
I have never been permitted to see two satellites in
conjunction when their distance from Jupiter was
great, whereas near Jupiter two, three, and sometimes
all (four), have been found closely packed together.
Moreover, it may be detected that the revolutions of

the satellites which describe the smallest circles round
Jupiter are the most rapid, for the satellites nearest
to Jupiter are often to be seen in the east, when the
day before they have appeared in the west, and contrariwise. Also the satellite moving in the greatest
orbit seems to me, after carefully weighing the
occasions of its returning to positions previously
noticed, to have a periodic time of half a month.[1]
Besides, we have a notable and splendid argument to
remove the scruples of those who can tolerate the
revolution of the planets round the Sun in the Copernican system, yet are so disturbed by the motion of
one Moon about the Earth, while both accomplish an
orbit of a year's length about the Sun, that they
consider that this theory of the constitution of the
universe must be upset as impossible; for now we
have not one planet only revolving about another,
while both traverse a vast orbit about the Sun, but
our sense of sight presents to us four satellites circling

---

[1] In the edition of Galileo's works published at Florence, 1854, there are
given the tables of the hourly movements of the satellites of Jupiter, from
which Galileo determined their periods of revolution. In the beginning
of his treatise on floating bodies, *Discorso intorno i Galleggianti*, 1611-12,
Galileo gives the times of rotation as approximately, (i.) 1 d. 18½ h. ;
(ii.) 3 d. 13½ h.; (iii.) 7 d. 4 h.; (iv.) 16 d. 18 h. ; he also published
configurations of the satellites calculated for March, April, and a part of
May 1613. The periodic times of the satellites, as corrected by later
observers, are, (i.) 1 d. 18 h. 28 m. ; (ii.) 3 d. 13 h. 15 m.; (iii.) 7 d.
3 h. 43 m. ; (iv.) 16 d. 16 h. 32 m.

about Jupiter, like the Moon about the Earth, while
the whole system travels over a mighty orbit about
the Sun in the space of twelve years.

Explanation
of the varia-
tions in
brightness
of Jupiter's
satellites. Lastly, I must not pass over the consideration of
the reason why it happens that the Medicean stars, in
performing very small revolutions about Jupiter,
seem sometimes more than twice as large as at other
times. We can by no means look for the explanation
in the mists of the Earth's atmosphere, for they appear
increased or diminished, while the discs of Jupiter
and neighbouring fixed stars are seen quite unaltered.
That they approach and recede from the Earth at the
points of their revolutions nearest to and furthest
from the Earth to such an extent as to account for so
great changes seems altogether untenable, for a strict
circular motion can by no means show those phenomena; and an elliptical motion (which in this case
would be nearly rectilinear) seems to be both untenable and by no means in harmony with the phenomena observed. But I gladly publish the explanation
which has occurred to me upon this subject, and
submit it to the judgment and criticism of all true
philosophers. It is certain that when atmospheric
mists intervene the Sun and Moon appear larger, but
the fixed stars and planets less than they really are;
hence the former luminaries, when near the horizon,
are larger than at other times, but stars appear

smaller, and are frequently scarcely visible ; also they are still more diminished if those mists are bathed in light; so stars appear very small by day and in the twilight, but the Moon does not appear so, as I have previously remarked. Moreover, it is certain that not only the Earth, but also the Moon, has its own vaporous sphere enveloping it, for the reasons which I have previously mentioned, and especially for those which shall be stated more fully in my *System;* and we may consistently decide that the same is true with regard to the rest of the planets ; so that it seems to be by no means an untenable opinion to place round Jupiter also an atmosphere denser than the rest of the ether,[1] about which, like the Moon about the sphere of the elements, the Medicean planets (Jupiter's satellites) revolve; and that by the intervention of this atmosphere they appear smaller when they are in apogee ; but when in perigee, through the absence or

---

[1] Modern astronomers agree in assigning an atmosphere to Jupiter, but consider it not extensive enough to affect the brightness of the satellites. —(WEBB, *Celestial Objects for Common Telescopes.*) Their absolute magnitudes are different, and their surfaces have been observed to be obscured by spots, which may account for the variations of their brightness. These spots, like the lunar spots, are probably due to variations of reflective power at different parts of their surfaces, for as they always turn the same face to Jupiter, they present different portions of their surfaces to us periodically, and it has been ascertained by observation that " these fluctuations in their brightness are periodical, depending on their position with respect to the Sun."—(HERSCHEL, *Outlines of Astronomy;* ARAGO, *Astronomie Populaire,* 1854.)

attenuation of that atmosphere, they appear larger. Want of time prevents my going further into these matters ; my readers may expect further remarks upon these subjects in a short time.

—————

Original Configurations of Jupiter's Satellites observed by Galileo in the months of January, February, and March 1610, *and published with the* 1st *edition of his book* SIDEREUS NUNCIUS, *Venice,* 1610.

FIG.	DATE.	EAST.	WEST.
1	Jan. 7	• • O	•
2	8	O • • •	
3	10	• • O	
4	11	• • O	
5	12	• •O	•
6	13	• O • • •	
7	15	O • • • •	
8	15	O • • •	
9	16	•O•	•
10	17	• O	•

Fig.	Date.	East.	West.
11	Jan. 17	• • O	•
12	18	• O	•
13	19	• O	• •
14	19	• • O	• •
15	20	• O	• •
16	20	• O • •	
17	20	• O • •	
18	21	• • • O	•
19	22	• O • •	•
20	22	• O	• • •
21	23	• • O	•
22	23	• O	
23	24	• • • O	
24	25	• • O	
25	26	• • O	•
26	26	• • O	•
27	27	• O	
28	30	• O • •	
29	31	• • O	•

Fig.	Date.	East.	West.
30	Jan. 31	• •˙ ○	•
31	Feb. 1	• •○	•
32	2	• ○ •	•
33	2	• • ○ •	•
34	3	• ○ •	•
35	4	• •○ •	•
36	4	• • ○ • •	
37	6	• ○ •	
38	7.	• • ○	
39	8	• • • ○	
40	9	• • ○ •	
41	10	• •○	
42	11	• • ○ •	
43	11	• • •○ •	
44	11	• • • ○ •	
45	12	• •○• •	
46	13	• • ○ • •	
47	15	• • •○	
48.	15	• •○	

Fig.	Date.	East.	West.
49	Feb. 15		
50	16		
51	17		
52	18		
53	18		
54	19		
55	21		
56	25		
57	26		
58	26		
59	26	⊙ Star.	
60	27	Star ⊙	
61	28	Star ⊙	
62	28		
63	Mar. 1	Star ⊙	
64	2		Star ⊙

A PART OF THE PREFACE TO
KEPLER'S DIOPTRICS

FORMING

A CONTINUATION OF GALILEO'S
SIDEREAL MESSENGER.

In the preface to Kepler's *Dioptrics* there are introduced letters of Galileo about the new and astonishing discoveries which he had made in the heavens by the aid of the telescope since the publication of his work, *The Sidereal Messenger*. The portion of the preface which refers to Galileo, containing these letters and Kepler's remarks upon them, is added here, as continuing the original account of Galileo's astronomical discoveries.

Extract from the Preface of Kepler's Dioptrics.
Augsburg, 1611.

"*The Sidereal Messenger*" of Galileo has been for a long time in everybody's hands, also my "*Discussion*, such as it is, *with this Messenger*," and my *Brief Narrative* in confirmation of Galileo's *Sidereal Messenger*, so any reader may briefly weigh the chief points of that *Messenger* and see the nature and the value of the discoveries made by the aid of the telescope, the theory of which I am intending to demonstrate in this treatise. Actual sight testified that there is a certain bright heavenly body which we call the Moon. It was demonstrated from the laws of optics that this body is round; also Astronomy, by

Kepler remarks on the importance of the application of the telescope to astronomical investigations as indicated by Galileo's discoveries, published in his *Sidereal Messenger*.

some arguments founded upon optics, had built up the conclusion that its distance from the earth is about sixty semi-diameters of the earth. Various spots showed themselves in that body; and the result was a dubious opinion among a few philosophers, derived from Hecatæus' account of the stories about the island of the Hyperboreans,[1] that the reflected images of mountains and valleys, sea and land, were seen there; but now the telescope places all these matters before our eyes in such a way that he must be an intellectual coward who, while enjoying such a view, still thinks that the matter is open to doubt. Nothing is more certain than that the southern parts of the moon teem with mountains, very many in number, and vast in size; and that the northern parts, inasmuch as they are lower, receive in most extensive lakes the water flowing down from the south. The conclusions which previously Pena published as disclosed by the aid of optics, started indeed from certain slight supports, rather than foundations, afforded by actual sight, but were proved by long arguments depending one upon another, so that they might be assigned to human reason rather than to sight; but now our very eyes, as if a new door of heaven had been opened, are led to the view of matters once hidden from them. But if it should please any one to exhaust the force of reason-

[1] *Diodorus Siculus, ii. 47.*

ing upon these new observations, who does not see how far the contemplation of nature will extend her boundaries, when we ask, " What is the use of the tracts of mountains and valleys, and the very wide expanse of seas in the moon ?" and " May not some creature less noble than man be imagined such as might inhabit those tracts ?"

With no less certainty also do we decide by the use of this instrument even that famous question, which, coeval with philosophy itself, is disputed to this day by the noblest intellects—I mean, " Whether the earth can move (as the theory of the Planets greatly requires) without the overthrow of all bodies that have weight, or the confusion of the motion of the elements ? For if the earth were banished from the centre of the universe, some fear lest the water should leave the orb of the earth and flow to the centre of the universe ; and yet we see that in the moon, as well as in the earth, there is a quantity of moisture occupying the sunken hollows of that globe ; and although this orb revolves actually in the ether, and outside the centres not merely of the universe, but even of our earth, yet the mass of water in the moon is not at all hindered from cleaving invariably to the orb of the moon, and tending to the centre of the body to which it belongs. So, by this instance of the pheno-

F

mena of the moon, the science of optics amends the received theory of mechanics, and confirms on this point my introduction to my *Commentaries upon the Motions of the Planet Mars.*[1]

The followers of the Samian philosophy (for I may use this epithet to designate the philosophy originated by the Samians, Pythagoras and Aristarchus) have a strong argument against the apparent immobility of the earth provided in the phenomena of the moon. For we are taught by optics that if any one of us was in the moon, to him the moon, his abode, would seem

---

[1] Kepler says in his introduction to his *Commentaries upon the Motions of the Planet Mars*, that the theory of gravitation depends on certain axioms, one of which is that "heavy bodies do not tend to the centre of the universe, supposing the earth to be placed there, because that point is the centre of the universe, but because it is the centre of the earth. So, wherever the earth be set, or whithersoever it be transported, heavy bodies have a continual tendency to it." Kepler's object in this work was to correct the methods for determining the apparent places of the planets according to the three theories then current—the Ptolemaic, the Copernican, and that of Tycho Brahe.

In 1593 the observed place of the planet Mars differed by nearly 5° from the place calculated for it. Kepler accordingly studied the motions of this planet, and "by most laborious demonstrations and discussions of many observations," arrived at the conclusions known as Kepler's first and second laws ; according to which the Copernican system of eccentric and epicycles was replaced by an ellipse whose centre and eccentricity were the same as the centre and eccentricity of the eccentric in the older method, and the Sun therefore was in one of the foci. Also the motion of the planet in its orbit was such that equal areas were described about the Sun by the radius vector of the planet in equal times.—KEPLER, *Astronomia Nova αἰτολογητός* (Prague), 1609.

quite immovable, but our earth and sun and all the
rest of the heavenly bodies movable ; for the conclusions of sight are thus related.

Pena has noticed how astronomers, using the prin-
ciples of optics, have by most laborious reasoning
removed the Milky Way from the elementary universe, where Aristotle had placed it, into the highest
region of the ether ; but now, by the aid of the telescope lately invented, the very eyes of astronomers
are conducted straight to a thorough survey of the
substance of the Milky Way ; and whoever enjoys
this sight is compelled to confess that the Milky
Way is nothing else but a mass of extremely small
stars.

Again, up to this time the nature of nebulous stars
had been entirely unknown ; but if the telescope be
directed to one of such nebulous balls, as Ptolemy calls
them, it again shows, as in the case of the Milky Way,
three or four very bright stars clustered very close
together.

Again, who without this instrument would have
believed that the number of the fixed stars was ten
times, or perhaps twenty times, more than that which
is given in Ptolemy's description of the fixed stars ?
And whence, pray, should we seek for conclusive
evidence about the end or boundary of this visible

universe, proving that it is actually the sphere of the fixed stars, and that there is nothing beyond, except from this very discovery by the telescope of this multitude of fixed stars, which is, as it were, the vaulting of the mobile universe? Again, how greatly an astronomer would go wrong in determining the magnitude of the fixed stars, except he should survey the stars all over again with a telescope, also may be seen in Galileo's treatise, and we will also hereafter produce in proof a letter from a German astronomer.

But no words can express my admiration of that chapter of the *Sidereal Messenger* where the story is told of the discovery, by the aid of a very highly finished telescope, of another world, as it were, in the planet Jupiter. The mind of the philosopher almost reels as he considers that there is a vast orb, which is equal in mass to fourteen orbs like the earth (unless on this point the telescope of Galileo shall shortly reveal something more exact than the measurements of Tycho Brahe) round which circle four moons, not unlike this moon of ours; the slowest revolving in the space of fourteen of our days, as Galileo has published; the next to this, by far the brightest of the four, in the space of eight days, as I detected in last April and May; the other two in still shorter periods. And here the reasoning of my *Commen-*

taries about the Planet Mars, applied to a similar case, induces me to conclude also that the actual orb of Jupiter rotates with very great rapidity, most certainly faster than once in the space of one of our days; so that this rotation of the mighty orb upon its own axis is accompanied wherever it goes by the perpetual circuits of those four moons. Moreover, this sun of ours, the common source of heat and light for this terrestrial world as well as for that world of Jupiter, which we consider to be of the angular magnitude of 30′ at most, there scarcely subtends more than 6′ or 7′, and is found again in the same position among the fixed stars, having completed the zodiac in the interval, after a period of twelve of our years.[1] Accordingly, the creatures which live on that orb of Jupiter, while they contemplate the very swift courses of those four moons among the fixed stars, while they behold them and the sun rising and setting day by day, would swear

---

[1] The degree of accuracy attained by Kepler and Galileo with their imperfect instruments will be appreciated by comparing these statements with the determinations of later astronomers. Jupiter is about 1300 times the size of the Earth. Its diameter is about 87,000 miles; time of rotation, 9 h. 55 m. 21 sec.; time of revolution, 4333 days nearly. The angular diameter of the sun, seen from Jupiter, is between 6′ and 7′. The times of revolution of the four satellites are, as already given: (i.) 1 d. 18 h. 28 m., (ii.) 3 d. 13 h. 15 m., (iii.) 7 d. 3 h. 43 m., (iv.) 16 d. 6 h. 32 m.

by Jupiter-in-stone, like the Romans (for I have lately
returned from those parts), that their orb of Jupiter
remains immovable in one spot, and that the fixed
stars and the sun, which are the bodies really at rest,
no less than those four moons of theirs, revolve round
that abode of theirs with manifold variety of motions.
And from this instance now, much more than before
from the instance of the moon, any follower of the
Samian philosophy will learn what reply may be made
to any one objecting to the theory of the motion of
the earth as absurd, and alleging the evidence of our
sight.   O telescope, instrument of much knowledge,
more precious than any sceptre !   Is not he who
holds thee in his hand made king and lord of the
works of God ?   Truly

> " All that is overhead, the mighty orbs
>   With all their motions, thou dost subjugate
>   To man's intelligence."

If there is any one in some degree friendly to Copernicus and the lights of the Samian philosophy, who
finds this difficulty only, that he doubts how it can
happen, supposing the earth to perform again and
again her course among the planets through the
ethereal plains, that the moon should keep so con-
stantly by her side, like an inseparable companion,
and at the same time fly round and round the actual

orb of the earth, just like a faithful dog which goes round and round his master on some journey, now running in front, now deviating to this side or that, in ever-varying mazes, let him look at the planet Jupiter, which, as this telescope shows, certainly carries in its train not one such companion only, like the earth, as Copernicus showed, but actually four, that never leave it, though all the time hastening each in its own orbit.

But enough has been said about these matters in my *Discussion with the Sidereal Messenger.* It is time that I should turn to those discoveries which have been made since the publication of Galileo's *Sidereal Messenger*, and since my *Discussion* with it, by means of this telescope.

It is now just a year since Galileo wrote to Prague, and gave full notice that he had detected something new in the heavens beyond his former discoveries; and that there might not be any one who, with the intention of detracting from his credit, should try to pass himself off as an earlier observer of the phenomenon, Galileo gave a certain space of time for the publication of the new phenomena which any one had seen; he himself meanwhile described his discovery in letters transposed in this manner: *s m a i s m r m i l m e p o e t a l e u m i b u n e n u g t t a u i r a s.* Out of these

Galileo's discovery of Saturn's ring (imperfectly).

letters I made an uncouth verse which I inserted in
my *Short Account* in the month of September of last
year :—

Salve umbistineum[1] geminatum Martia proles.

Hail, twin companionship, children of Mars.

But I was a very long way from the meaning of
the letters; it contained nothing to do with Mars;
and, not to detain you, reader, here is the solution of
the·riddle in the words of Galileo himself, the author
of it :[2]—

" *Di Firenze li* 13 *di Novembre* 1610.—Ma passando ad altro, giacchè il Sig. Keplero ha in questa sua
ultima narrazione stampate le lettere che io mandai
trasposte a Vostra Signoria Illustrissima e Reverendissima venendomi anco significato come Sua Maestà
ne desidera il senso, ecco che io lo mando a Vostra
Signoria Illustrissima per participarlo con Sua Maestà
col Sig. Keplero e con chi piacerà a Vostra Signoria
Illustrissima bramando io che lo sappia ognuno.   Le

---

[1] *Umbistineum.* Apparently this is some German word with a Latin
ending, such as *um-bei-stehn;* Kepler fancied that Galileo had discovered
two satellites of Mars.

[2] The text of the four letters of Galileo followed here is that given in
the edition of Galileo's works published at Florence, 1842-56 ; that in
the edition of Kepler's *Dioptrics*, published at Augsburg, 1611, is very
inaccurate.   These letters were written to Giuliano de' Medici, ambassador of the Grand-Duke of Tuscany to the Emperor Rudolf II. at Prague.

lettere dunque combinate nel lor vero senso dicono così,

Altissimum planetam tergeminum observavi.

Questo è, che Saturno con mia grandissima ammirazione ho osservato essere non una stella sola, ma tre insieme, le quali quasi si toccano; e sono trà di loro totalmente immobili, e constituite in questa guisa oOo. Quella di mezzo è assai più grande delle laterali; sono situate una da oriente, l'altra da occidente, nella medesima linea retta a capello; non sono giustamente secondo la dirittura del Zodiaco, ma l'occidentale si eleva alquanto verso Borea; forse sono parallele all' Equinoziale. Se si guarderanno con un occhiale che non sia di grandissima moltiplicazione, non appariranno tre stelle ben distinte, ma parrà, che Saturno sia una stella lunghetta in forma di un' oliva, così, ◯. Ma servendosi di un occhiale che moltiplichi più di mille volte in superficie, si vedranno tre globi distintissimi, che quasi si toccano, non apparendo trà essi maggior divisione di un sottil filo oscuro. Or ecco trovata la corte a Giove, e due Servi a questo Vecchio che l'aiutano a camminare nè mai se gli staccano dal fianco. Intorno agli altri Pianeti non ci è novità alcuna, ec."

Although these words differ little from Latin, yet I will translate them that no difficulty may hinder my

reader from following me. Thus then Galileo writes:
—"But to come now to my second topic. Since
Kepler has published in that recent '*Narrative*' of
his the letters which I sent as an anagram to your
illustrious Lordship, and since an intimation has been
given me that his Majesty desires to be taught the
meaning of those letters, I send it to your illustrious
Lordship, that your Lordship may communicate it to
his Majesty, to Kepler, and to any one your Lordship
may wish.

"The letters when joined together as they ought to
be, say this,

> ' Altissimum planetam tergeminum observavi,'
> ' I have observed the most distant of the planets to have a triple
> form.'

"For in truth I have found out with the most intense surprise that the planet Saturn is not merely
one single star, but three stars very close together,
so much so that they are all but in contact one
with another. They are quite immovable with
regard to each other, and are arranged in this manner, oOo. The middle star of the three is by far
greater than the two on either side. They are situated one towards the east, the other towards the
west, in one straight line to a hair's-breadth; not, however, exactly in the direction of the Zodiac, for the

star furthest to the west rises somewhat towards the
north; perhaps they are parallel to the equator. If
you look at them through a glass that does not
multiply much, the stars will not appear clearly
separate from one another, but Saturn's orb will
appear somewhat elongated, of the shape of an olive,
thus, ⬭. But if you should use a glass which multi-
plies a surface more than a thousand times, there will
appear very distinctly three orbs, almost touching
one another; and they will be thought to be not
further apart than the breadth of a very fine and
scarcely visible thread. So you see a guard of satellites has been found for Jupiter, and for the decrepit
little old man two servants to help his steps and never
leave his side. Concerning the rest of the planets I
have found nothing new."

So says Galileo; but if I may do so, I will not
make an old dotard out of Saturn, and two servants for him out of his companion orbs, but rather out
of those three united bodies I will make a triple Geryon,
out of Galileo Hercules, and out of the telescope
his club, armed with which, Galileo has conquered
that most distant of the planets, drawn it out of
the furthest recesses of nature, dragged it down to
earth, and exposed it to the gaze of us all. It pleases
me too, now that the nest has been found, to consider

cause the sun, which appears there only asBut I must draw in the reins and check my mind in

[1] Virgil, *Eclog.* iii. 105.

different from the first account, something changed in course of time.[1]

At the end of his letter Galileo seemed to think that he had come to the end of his reports about the planets, and observations of new phenomena respecting them, but ever on the watch, that eye of his, that one not of Nature's making—I mean his telescope—in a short time made more discoveries, concerning which read the following letter of Galileo:—

"*Di Firenze li* 11 *di Decembre* 1610.—Sto con desiderio, attendendo la risposta a due mie scritte ultimamente per sentire quello, che averà detto il Sig.

Account of Galileo's discovery of the phases of Venus.

---

[1] The completion of Galileo's observations on Saturn depended on the improvement of astronomical instruments, as will be evident from the following sketch. Galileo made out the first indications of Saturn's ring in 1610, as narrated in his letter, with a power of thirty; but in December 1612 he wrote to one of his friends, Marco Velseri, that he could no longer see these indications, and began to imagine that his telescope had deceived him, and apparently abandoned further researches. Hevelius in 1642 saw the ring more clearly, but figured it as two crescents attached to Saturn by their cusps. At length, in 1653, Huyghens provided himself with a power of one hundred, having made the lenses with his own hands, and immediately discovered the explanation of the phenomena which had baffled previous observers. He published his explanation of Saturn's ring, and his discovery of the first satellite, in his *Systema Saturnium,* 1659. Cassini, with still more powerful instruments, discovered four more satellites in 1671, 1672, 1684. Sir William Herschel in 1789 detected two more, " which can only be seen with telescopes of extraordinary power and perfection, and under the most favourable atmospheric circumstances."—(HERSCHEL, *Outlines of Astronomy,* § 548.) And the last of the eight satellites was discovered in 1848 by Lassell of Liverpool, and Bond of Cambridge, U.S., simultaneously.

Keplero della stravaganza di Saturno. Intanto mando [a Vostra Signoria Illustrissima e Reverendissima] la cifra di un altro particolare osservato da me nuovamente, il quale si tira dietro la decisione di grandissime controversie in Astronomia, ed in particolare contiene in se un gagliardo argomento per la constitutione [Pitagorica e Copernicana] dell' Universo ; e a suo tempo pubblicherò la deciferazione ed altri particolari. Spero che averò trovato il metodo per definire i periodi dei quattro Pianeti Medicei, stimati con gran ragione quasi inesplicabili dal Sig. Keplero, al quale piacerà, ec.

"Le lettere trasposte sono queste :

"Haec immatura a me jam frustra leguntur, o.y."

Which may be translated thus :—

" I am anxiously looking for an answer to my last two letters, that I may learn what Kepler says about the marvels of Saturn's orb. In the meantime I send him a riddle concerning a certain new and splendid observation which tends to decide great controversies in astronomy; and especially contains a fine argument in favour of the Pythagorean and Copernican system of the universe. At the proper time I will publish the solution of the riddle, and some other particulars. I hope that I have found a method of determining the periodic times of the four Medicean planets, which

Kepler, not without very good reason, thought inexplicable, etc.

" The letters turned into an anagram, are these :

" Haec immatura a me jam frustra leguntur, o.y."

So far Galileo. But if, reader, this letter has filled you with a desire to know the meaning contained in those letters, then you must read another letter of Galileo which follows.

But before you do so, I should like you to notice, by the way, what Galileo says about the Pythagorean and Copernican system of the universe. For he points to my *Mystery of the Universe*,[1] published fourteen years ago, in which I took the dimensions of the Planetary orbits according to the astronomy of Copernicus, who makes the sun immovable in the centre, and the earth

---

[1] Kepler, in his *Mystery of the Universe*, endeavoured to connect the orbits of the planets with the five regular solids, thus : If in a sphere (i.) a cube be inscribed, and in the cube a sphere (ii.); and in that sphere a tetrahedron, and in the tetrahedron a sphere (iii.); and in that sphere a dodecahedron, and in the dodecahedron a sphere (iv.); and in that sphere an icosahedron, and in the icosahedron a sphere (v.); and in that sphere an octahedron, and in the octahedron a sphere (vi.), the diameters of these six spheres will be proportional to the diameters of the orbits of Saturn, Jupiter, Mars, the Earth, Venus, and Mercury respectively ; or, as Kepler expresses it, the common centre of these spheres represents the position of the Sun, and the six spheres represent the spheres of the planets.

By these considerations, however, Kepler was led to enunciate his third law, that the squares of the periodic times of planets are proportional to the cubes of their mean distances from the sun.—KEPLER, *Prodromus Dissertationum Mathematicarum continens Mysterium Cosmographicum, etc.* (Tübingen, 1596.)

movable both round the sun and upon its own axis;
and I showed that the differences of their orbits cor-
responded to the five regular Pythagorean figures, which
had been already distributed by their author among
the elements of the world, though the attempt was
admirable rather than happy or legitimate, and for
which figures' sake Euclid wrote the whole of his
Geometry.   Now, in that *Mystery* you may find a sort
of combination of Astronomy and Euclid's Geometry,
and through this combination a most thorough completion and finishing of them both; and this was the
reason why I waited with intense longing to see what
sort of an argument Galileo would produce in favour
of the Pythagorean system of the universe.   After
this explanation, Galileo's letter about this argument
was as follows :—

" Illustrissimo e Reverendissimo Signore mio colen-
dissimo.

"E tempo che io deciferi a Vostra Signoria Illustrissima e Reverendissima e per lei al Sig. Keplero le
lettere trasposte le quali alcune settimane sono le
inviai ; è tempo dico, giacchè sono interamente chiaro
della verità del fatto, sicchè non ci resta un minimo
scrupolo, o dubbio. Sapranno dunque come circa a
tre mesi fa vedendosi Venere vespertina la comin-
ciai ad osservar diligentemente coll' occhiale, per

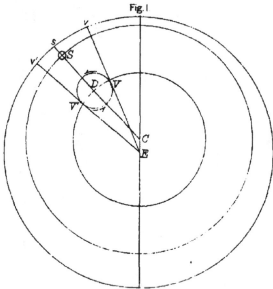

Fig. 1

E the Earth (centre of universe). S the Sun C centre of eccentric. D centre of planet's epicycle V V stationary points. s v v' projections of SVV' on the ecliptic of which E is the centre.

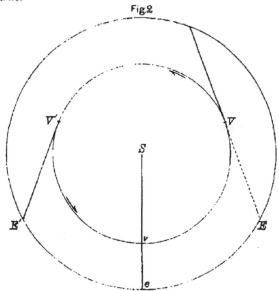

Fig. 2

S the Sun, centre of solar system. v e positions of planet and Earth at conjunction VV' stationary points of planet EE' corresponding positions of the Earth.

veder col senso stesso quello di che non dubitava punto l'intelletto. La vidi dunque sul principio di figura rotonda, pulita e terminata, ma molto picciola ; di tal figura si mantenne sino che cominciò ad avvicinarsi alla sua massima digressione, ma tra tanto andò crescendo in mole. Cominciò poi a mancare dalla rotondità nella sua parte orientale ed avversa al Sole, e in pochi giorni si ridusse ad esser un mezzo cerchio perfettissimo, e tale si mantenne, senza punto alterarsi, finchè incominciò à ritirarsi verso il .Sole, allontanandosi dalla tangente. Ora va calando dal mezzo cerchio, e si mostra cornicolata, e anderà assottigliandosi sino all' occultazione, riducendosi allora con corna sottilissime. Quindi passando all' apparizione mattutina, la vedremo pur falcata, e sottilissima e colle corna avverse al Sole ; anderà poi crescendo fino alla massima digressione, dove apparirà semicircolare, e tale senza alterarsi si manterrà molti giorni, e poi dal mezzo cerchio passerà presto al tutto tondo, e così rotonda si conserverà poi per molti mesi. Il suo diametro adesso è circa cinque volte maggiore di quello, che si mostrava nella sua prima apparizione vespertina ; dalla quale mirabile esperienza abbiamo sensata, e certa dimostrazione di due gran questioni state fin qui dubbie trà i maggiori ingegni del Mondo. L'una è, che i Pianeti tutti son di lor natura tenebrosi (accadendo anco a Mercurio l'istesso, che a Venere). L'altra, che Venere necessarissimamente si volge intorno al Sole, come anco Mercurio, cosa, che degli altri Pianeti, fu creduta da' Pitagorici, dal Copernico, dal Keplero e da' loro seguaci, ma non sensatamente provata, come ora in Venere, ed in Mercurio.

"Averanno dunque il Sig. Keplero, e gli altri Copernicani da gloriarsi di aver creduto e filosofato bene, sebbene ci è toccato, e ci è per toccare ancora ad esser reputati dall' università dei Filosofi in libris, per poco intendenti, e poco meno che stolti.

"Le parole dunque, che mandai trasposte, e che dicevano,

Haec immatura a me jam frustra leguntur, o.y.

dicono ordinate

Cynthiae figuras aemulatur mater amorum.

Cioè, che Venere imita le figure della Luna. Osservai tre notti sono l'ecclisse, nella quale non vi è cosa notabile, solo si vede il taglio dell' ombra indistinto, confuso e come annebbiato, e questo per derivare essa ombra dalla Terra lontanissima da essa Luna. Voleva scrivere altri particolari, ma essendo stato trattenuto molto da alcuni gentiluomini, ed essendo l'ora tardissima, son forzato a finire. Favoriscami salutare in mio nome i SS. Keplero, Asdale e Segheti, ed a Vostra Signoria Illustrissima con ogni reverenza bacio le

mani, e dal Signore Dio gli prego felicità. Di Firenze
il primo di Gennaio 1610. Ab Incarnatione.

"Di Vostra Signoria Illustrissima e Reverendissima
Servidore obbligatissimo. GALILEO GALILEI."

Such is Galileo's letter; but let me give you the
substance of it :—

"It is time for me to disclose the method of reading
the letters which some weeks since I sent you as an
anagram. It is time now, I mean, after I have
become quite certain about the matter, so much so
that I have no longer even a shadow of doubt. You
must know then that about three months ago, when
the star of Venus could be seen, I began to look at it
through a telescope with great attention, so that I
might grasp with my physical senses an idea which I
was entertaining as certain. At first then you must
know the planet Venus appeared of a perfectly
circular form, accurately so, and bounded by a
distinct edge, but very small; this figure Venus kept
until it began to approach its greatest distance from
the sun, and meanwhile the apparent size of its orb
kept on increasing. From that time it began to lose
its roundness on the eastern side, which was turned
away from the sun, and in a few days it contracted
its visible portion into an exact semicircle; that

figure lasted without the smallest alteration until it began to return towards the sun where it leaves the tangent drawn to its epicycle.[1] At this time it loses the semicircular form more and more, and keeps on diminishing that figure until its conjunction, when it will wane to a very thin crescent. After completing its passage past the sun, it will appear to us, at its

---

[1] In the Ptolemaic system the earth's centre was regarded as the centre of the universe, and the movements of the heavenly bodies were explained by eccentrics and epicycles. The sun was conceived to describe a circle about a point not exactly coinciding with the centre of the earth, called the sun's *eccentric.* The planets described epicycles (circles) whose centres described eccentrics (circles), and the centres of these eccentrics coincided with the centre of the sun's eccentric. In the case of Mercury and Venus the centre of the epicycle was always on the line drawn from the centre of the eccentric to the sun's centre. In the case of the other planets the construction was more complicated. The stationary points were determined by drawing tangents from the earth's centre (or the observer) to the epicycle, as in the figure (1).—(GASSENDI, *Institutio Astronomica,* 1647.) This will explain Kepler's description of the stationary points as the points where the planet leaves the tangent to its epicycle, supposing that he uses the terms of the current (*i.e.* Ptolemaic) astronomy. Copernicus placed the sun instead of the earth at the centre of the universe, but to determine the positions of the planets at any given time with as much accuracy as was attainable with the Ptolemaic system, he was obliged to use a similar method of eccentrics and epicycles, so that Kepler's expression may be understood to describe the stationary points according to the Copernican theory, though it is still strange that he should not recognise the elliptical form of the planetary orbits, which he had lately demonstrated after most laborious reasoning in his *Commentaries on the Motion of the Planet Mars,* 1609. Galileo's own expression seems to describe the stationary points according to the Copernican system, as would be expected, as the points where the planet leaves the tangent drawn to its *orbit* from the earth (Fig. 2).

appearance as a morning star, as only sickle-shaped, turning a very thin crescent away from the sun; afterwards the crescent will fill up more and more until the planet reaches its greatest distance from the sun, in which position it will appear semicircular, and that figure will last for many days without appreciable variation. Then by degrees, from being semicircular it will change to a full orb, and will keep that perfectly circular figure for several months; but at this instant the diameter of the orb of Venus is about five times as large as that which it showed at its first appearance as an evening star.

"From the observation of these wonderful phenomena we are supplied with a determination most conclusive, and appealing to the evidence of our senses, of two very important problems, which up to this day were discussed by the greatest intellects with different conclusions. One is that the planets are bodies not self-luminous (if we may entertain the same views about Mercury as we do about Venus). The second is that we are absolutely compelled to say that Venus (and Mercury also) revolves round the sun, as do also all the rest of the planets. A truth believed indeed by the Pythagorean school, by Copernicus, and by Kepler, but never proved by the evidence of our senses, as it is now proved in the case of Venus and

Mercury. Kepler therefore and the rest of the school of Copernicus have good reason for boasting that they have shown themselves good philosophers, and that their belief was not devoid of foundation ; however much it has been their lot, and may even hereafter be their lot, to be regarded by the philosophers of our times, who philosophise on paper, with an universal agreement, as men of no intellect, and little better than absolute fools.

" The words which I sent with their letters transposed, and which said,

Haec immatura a me jam frustra leguntur, o.y.

when reduced to their proper order, read thus,

Cynthiae figuras aemulatur mater amorum :
The mother of the Loves rivals the phases of Cynthia :

that is,

Venus imitates the phases of the Moon.

Three days ago I observed an eclipse of the moon, but not anything worthy of special notice occurred in it. Only the edge of the shadow appeared indistinct, blurred, and hazy ; the cause of the phenomenon no doubt is that the shadow has its origin at the earth, at a great distance from the body of the moon.

" I have some other particulars, but I am prevented by time from writing about them, etc."

So writes Galileo.

What now, dear reader, shall we make out of our telescope ?   Shall we make a Mercury's magic-wand to cross the liquid ether with, and, like Lucian,[1] lead a colony to the uninhabited evening star, allured by the sweetness of the place ? or shall we make it a Cupid's arrow, which, entering by our eyes, has pierced our inmost mind, and fired us with a love of Venus ? For what language is too strong for the marvellous beauty of this orb, if, having no light of its own, it can attain simply by the borrowed light of the sun to such splendour, as Jupiter has not, nor the moon, though enjoying a proximity to the sun as close as Venus ; for if the moon's light be compared with the light of Venus, it will be seen to be certainly greater on account of the apparent magnitude of the moon, but, in comparison with the light of Venus, dull, dead, and leaden.   O truly golden Venus ! Will any one doubt any more that the whole orb of Venus is wrought most smoothly out of pure unalloyed gold, since its surface, when only placed in the sunlight, reflects a splendour so intense ! And here let me add my experiments about the alteration of the light of Venus on blinking the eye, which I have examined in the part of my Astronomy which

---

[1] Lucian, *Ver. Hist.* i. 12.

treats of Optics.   Reasoning will be able to conclude
nothing else but this, that the orb of Venus turns on
its own axis with an exceedingly swift rotation, dis-
playing one after another different parts of its surface
which are more or less capable of retaining the sun's
light.[1]

.   .   .   .

But enough of my own conclusions.   Let us now
hear as an epilogue Galileo's conclusions built up out
of all the observations which he has made with his
telescope, and announced from time to time.   Thus
he writes once more :—

Galileo's con-
clusions with
regard to the
inherent
nature of the
brightness of
the stars.

" Illustrissimo e Reverendissimo Signore mio colen-
dissimo.

"Ho ricevuto gusto, e contento particolarissimo nella
lettura dell' ultima di Vostra Signoria Illustrissima
e Reverendissima delli 7 stante, ed in particolare in
quella parte dove ella m'accenna la favorevole in-
clinazione dell' Illustriss. Sig. Cons. Wackher, verso

---

[1] The first scientific determination of the period of the rotation of
Venus was made by Dominique Cassini in 1666, from observations of
spots on the planet, and concluded to be about 24 hours; but in 1726
Bianchini deduced a period of 24 d. 8 h. from similar observations.   The
true period is considered to be 23 h. 21 m., determined by Schroeter
by a series of observations lasting from 1788 to 1793 on the periodicity
of the deformation of the horns of Venus.—(ARAGO, *Astronomie Populaire*,
1854.)

Kepler's statements can only be regarded as anticipations of phenomena
not yet actually observed.

di me, la quale io infinitamente stimo, ed apprezzo ;
e poichè quella ha principalmente origine dall' aver
io incontrate osservazioni necessariamente dimostranti
conclusioni per avanti tenute vere da sua Signoria
Illustrissima per confermarmi maggiormente il pos-
sesso di grazia tanto pregiata da me, prego Vostra
Signoria Illustrissima e Reverendissima a fargli in-
tendere per mia parte come conforme alla credenza di
Sua Signoria Illustrissima ho dimostrazione certa, che
siccome tutti i Pianeti ricevono il lume dal Sole,
essendo per se stessi tenebrosi, e opachi; così le
Stelle fisse risplendono per lor natura, non bisognose
dell' illustrazione de' raggi solari, li quali, Dio sa, se
arrivino a tanta altezza, più di quello, che arrivi a noi
il lume di una di esse fisse. Il principal fondamento
del mio discorso è nell' osservare io molto evidente-
mente con gli occhiali che quei Pianeti di mano in
mano, che si trovano più vicini a noi, o al Sole,
ricevono maggiore splendore, e più illustremente ce
lo riverberano ; e perciò Marte perigeo, e a noi vicin-
issimo si vede assai più splendido, che Giove ; benchè
a quello di mole assai inferiore ; e difficilmente se gli
può coll' occhiale levare quella irradiazione, che im-
pedisce il vedere il suo disco terminato, e rotondo ; il
che in Giove non accade, vedendosi esquisitamente
circolare. Saturno poi per la sua gran lontananza si

vede esattamente terminato, sì la Stella maggiore di mezzo, come le due piccole laterali ; ed appare il suo lume languido, ed abbacinato e senza niuna irradiazione, che impedisca il distinguere i suoi tre piccoli globi terminatissimi. Ora poichè apertamente veggiamo, che il Sole molto splendidamente illustra Marte vicino, e che molto più languido è il lume di Giove (sebbene senza lo strumento appare assai chiaro, il che accade per la grandezza, e candore della Stella) languidissimo, e fosco quello di Saturno, come molto più lontano, quali doveriano apparirci le Stelle fisse lontane indicibilmente più di Saturno, quando il lume loro derivasse dal Sole ? Certamente debolissime, torbide e smorte. Ma tutto l'opposito si vede, perocchè se rimireremo per esempio il Cane, incontreremo un fulgore vivissimo, che quasi ci toglie la vista, con una vibrazione di raggi tanto fiera, e possente, che in comparazione di quello rimangono i Pianeti, e dico Giove e Venere stessa, come un impurissimo vetro appresso un limpidissimo e finissimo diamante. E benchè il disco di esso Cane apparisca non maggiore della cinquantesima parte di quello di Giove, tuttavia la sua irradiazione è grande, e fiera in modo, che l'istesso globo tra i proprii crini s'implica, e quasi si perde, e con qualche difficoltà si distingue ; dove che Giove (e molto più Saturno) si vedono e terminati, e di una luce languida, e per così dire quieta. E per tanto io stimo, che bene filosoferemo, referendo la causa della scintillazione delle Stelle fisse, al vibrare, che elle fanno dello splendore proprio e nativo dall' intima loro sustanza ; dove che nella superficie de' Pianeti termina più presto, e si finisce l'illuminazione, che dal Sole deriva, e si parte. Se io sentirò qualche particolare questione ricevuta dal medesimo Sig. Wackher, non resterò d' affaticarmivi intorno, per dimostrarmi, quale io sono desiderosissimo di servire un tanto Signore, e non già con isperanza di aggiungere al termine conseguito dal suo discorso, perchè benissimo comprendo, che a quanto sia passato per lo finissimo cribro del giudizio di esso, e del Sig. Keplero, non si può aggiungere di squisitezza ; nè io pretenderei altro, che col dubitare, e mal filosofare, eccitar loro al ritrovamento di nuove sottigliezze. Gl' ingegni singolari, che in gran numero fioriscono nell' Alemagna, mi hanno lungo tempo tenuto in desiderio di vederla, il qual desiderio ora si raddoppia per la nuova grazia dell' Illustrissimo Sig. Wackher, la quale mi farebbe divenir grande ogni picciola occasione, che mi si presentasse. Ma ho di soverchio occupata Vostra Signoria Illustrissima e Reverendissima. Degnisi per fine di offerirmi e dedi-carmi devotissimo servidore all' Illustrissimo Sig. Wackher, salutando anco caramente il Sig. Keplero,

ed a lei con ogni riverenza bacio le mani, e dal Signore
Dio le prego somma felicità.

"[Di Firenze li 26] di Marzo 1611.   Di Vostra
Signoria Illustrissima e Reverendissima obbligatissimo
Servidore,   GALILEO GALILEI."

When translated, the meaning is as follows:—

" Your last letter has exceedingly pleased me,
especially that part which assures me of the friendly
feeling entertained towards me by the most illustrious Imperial Counsellor, Wagher, which I for my
part highly appreciate.   And since the cause of this
friendliness is, that I have incontestably demonstrated by some observations of mine certain conclusions which he had long held as true, I wish to
confirm my possession of favour, which I value so
much, and accordingly I ask you to give him this
piece of news from me; that I have most conclusive
arguments ready, showing clearly that, just as he
holds, all the planets receive their light from the
sun, being by constitution bodies dark and devoid
of light;[1] but that the fixed stars shine by their own
proper light, not needing to be illuminated by the

---

[1] Proctor (*Other Worlds than Ours*, 1875) has given some reasons for
believing that Jupiter and Saturn shine in part with their own light,
owing to their great internal heat.

sun's rays, since God knows whether they reach the very remote region of the fixed stars with intensity even equal to the small intensity with which the rays of the fixed stars come down to us.

"My demonstration depends chiefly on this fact, that with the telescope I have distinctly observed that the planets receive greater brightness, and reflect it more intensely, in proportion as each one is nearer to us and to the sun. So Mars in perigee, that is, when nearest to the earth, greatly surpasses Jupiter in brightness, although in actual size it is far inferior to Jupiter; and in consequence it is difficult to receive the effulgence of this planet in the telescope, for it is so great as to prevent the eye from being able to distinguish the circular termination of the planet's disc. This does not happen in the case of Jupiter, for it appears quite circular. The next planet, Saturn, on account of its great distance likewise—for indeed it is the most remote of the planets,—appears bounded by a well-defined edge, both the greater orb in the middle and the two small orbs at its sides. Indeed, it appears to shine with a faint and delicate light, without any effulgence to prevent an observer recognising the well-defined termination of its three orbs. Since, then, we see that Mars, the nearest of the three, is illumined by the sun with very great splendour, and that the light of Jupiter, at a greater distance, is much more faint (although without the use of an instrument it appears tolerably bright, which is due to the size and brilliancy of its body), and that the light of Saturn, at the greatest distance, is most faint, and almost watery, of what kind, do you think, would appear the light of the fixed stars, which are at an immeasurable distance further from the sun than Saturn, if they only received light from the sun? Most certainly, extremely feeble, indistinct, and pallid. And yet we find quite the contrary; for, let us look with our eyes at the Dog-Star, for example. We shall encounter a most vivid brilliancy, which almost pricks the eye with the rapid sparkling of its rays, of such intensity that, in comparison with it, the planets, even Jupiter, and Venus too, are as thoroughly outshone as common and bad glass compared with a highly polished and most sparkling diamond. And although the orb of the Dog-Star appears no larger than the fiftieth part of Jupiter's disc, nevertheless its brilliancy is great and very strong; so that the form of its disc, which you expect to see, hides itself among the rays of its own refulgence, envelops itself in them, and almost disappears; and it is not distinguished without some difficulty from the rays which surround it. Whereas Jupiter, and still more Saturn, are seen well

defined ; and their light is without intensity, and, if
I may say so, quiescent. Wherefore I think that we
shall rightly apply our philosophy if we refer the cause
of the twinkling of the fixed stars to vibrations of a
brilliancy, which is their own, belonging to their constitution, and inherent in their substance, and say, on
the other hand, that the illumination of the planets,
which is derived from the sun, and distributed to the
world, is limited to their surface."

These are the scientific conclusions in Galileo's
letter ; the rest I omit.

You see then, studious reader, how the subtle mind
of Galileo, in my opinion the first philosopher of the
day, uses this telescope of ours like a sort of ladder,
scales the furthest and loftiest walls of the visible
world, surveys all things with his own eyes, and, from
the position he has gained, darts the glances of his
most acute intellect upon these petty abodes of ours—
the planetary spheres I mean,—and compares with
keenest reasoning the distant with the near, the lofty
with the deep.

VALE ET DEUM IN OPERIBUS SUIS CELEBRARE NUNQUAM DESINE.
KEPLER, *Narratio.*